KNOW
YOUR
BIBLE

OTHER JOSH McDOWELL BOOKS

FOR MORE INFORMATION about the ministry of
Campus Crusade for Christ, write to:

United Kingdom:
Campus Crusade for
Christ
4 Temple Row
Birmingham B2 5HG

Australia:
LIFE
PO Box A399
Sydney South 2000

Canada:
Campus Crusade for
Christ
Box 300
Vancouver,
BC V6C 2X3

New Zealand:
Lay Institute for
Evangelism
PO Box 8786
Auckland 3

West Africa:
Great Commission
Movement of
Nigeria
PO Box 500
Jos, Plateau State
Nigeria

Republic of South Africa:
Life Ministry
PO Box/Bus 91015
Auckland Park 2006

USA:
Campus Crusade for
Christ International
Arrowhead Springs,
San Bernardino, CA
92414

Ireland:
Campus Crusade for
Christ
264 Merrion Road
Dublin 4

KNOW YOUR BIBLE

JOSH MCDOWELL

Scripture Press

AMERSHAM-ON-THE-HILL, BUCKS HP6 6JQ, ENGLAND

Originally published as *Guide To Understanding Your Bible*

This British edition 1990

ISBN 1 872059 08 2

Production and Printing in England for
SCRIPTURE PRESS FOUNDATION (UK) LTD
Raans Road, Amersham-on-the-Hill, Bucks HP6 6JQ by
Nuprint Ltd, 30b Station Road, Harpenden, Herts AL5 4SE.

Dedicated
to the
staff, translators, families,
and financial supporters of
Wycliffe Bible Translators,
whose lives, work, and sacrifice
have demonstrated the
supreme value of knowing and
understanding God's Word

CONTENTS

STEP FOUR Interpretation—"Know It"

STEP FIVE Application—"Do It"

APPENDIX

▼ STEP ONE ▼
The Right Mind-Set

▼ *CHAPTER ONE* ▼

A Fascinating Book

Have you ever wanted to know the Bible so well that the Holy Spirit could bring it to your mind quickly whenever you needed the insight it can give, the inspiration it contains, or the guidance available through its precepts?

"Yes," you say, "but that's not possible. I simply do not have that good a memory." I can understand your feelings, because at one time I felt the same. Yet through the years, I have been able to develop and use a method of Bible study that has given me a tremendous storehouse of biblical knowledge that I can recall even when I can't look at a Bible, such as when I am driving a car.

What is the key to gaining such a grounding in the Word of God? No, it is not a time-consuming program of Bible memorization, as profitable as memorizing the Bible is for us all. Instead, I recommend consistent use of the method of Bible study outlined in this book along with your Bible memory program. It will help you understand and remember biblical content, yet you do not have to spend hours at a time to use it profitably.

Did I hear someone say, "Oh, no, not another fancy system that is supposed to train me to absorb Scripture!" If that is your reaction, put your mind at ease. This method is designed to let you absorb the content of Scripture in such a simple and straightforward way that you will enjoy it. Yes, it is work—

nothing worthwhile comes without effort. But your effort will be richly rewarded as you grow in the knowledge of God as He reveals Himself in the Bible.

The benefits of systematic Bible study go far beyond those I have briefly outlined, however. David the psalmist put it beautifully: "The law of the LORD is perfect, restoring the soul; the testimony of the LORD is sure, making wise the simple. The precepts of the LORD are right, rejoicing the heart; the commandment of the LORD is pure, enlightening the eyes" (Psalm 19:7-8).

People have preached the Bible, taught it, cursed it, bought it, sold it, believed it, mocked it, and many have died for it. The Word of God offers to deliver more than we can ever possibly apply in one lifetime.

All this comes from a book that claims to be true, unique, without error, inspired by the living God, profitable, helpful in correction and reproof—a guidebook for living.

- UNIQUENESS OF THE BIBLE

The Bible's uniqueness, although not proving it is true, lends credibility to its claim to being true. For that many authors to agree on what is true is a remarkable achievement. Consider:

1. Written over a 1,500-year span.
2. Written over 40 generations.
3. Written by over 40 authors from every walk of life, including kings, peasants, philosophers, fishermen, poets, statesmen and scholars. Some of these are:
   > Moses, a political leader, trained in the universities of Egypt
   > Peter, a fisherman
   > Amos, a herdsman
   > Joshua, a military general
   > Nehemiah, a cupbearer
   > Daniel, a prime minister
   > Luke, a doctor
   > Solomon, a king
   > Matthew, a tax collector
   > Paul, a rabbi

4. Written in different places:
    Moses in the wilderness
    Jeremiah in a dungeon
    Daniel on a hillside and in a palace
    Paul inside prison walls
    Luke while traveling
    John on the Isle of Patmos
    Others in the rigors of a military campaign
5. Written at different times:
    David in times of war
    Solomon in times of peace
6. Written during different moods, some writing from the heights of joy, and others writing from the depths of sorrow and despair:
    The psalmists from a wide variety of feelings
    Jeremiah in great heaviness of heart
    Paul in sorrow, and in joy
7. Written on three continents:
    Asia, Africa, and Europe
8. Written in three languages:
    Hebrew: The language of the major part of the Old Testament. In 2 Kings 18:26-28 it was called "Judean"; in Isaiah 19:18, "the language of Canaan."
    Aramaic: The common language of the Near East until the time of Alexander the Great (6th century B.C.—4th century B.C.) in which portions of the Old Testament were written, i.e., most of Daniel 2-7.
    Greek: The language of the New Testament. It was the international language at the time of Christ.
9. Its subject matter includes hundreds of controversial subjects. A controversial subject is one that creates opposing opinions when mentioned or discussed.
    Biblical authors spoke on these subjects with harmony and continuity from Genesis to Revelation. There is one unfolding story: "God's redemption of man."
10. Unity of the Scriptures:

A FASCINATING BOOK

A representative of the *Great Books of the Western World* came to a friend's house to try to recruit salesmen for their series. I was there at the time. The agent spread out a chart of the *Great Books of the Western World* and spent five minutes talking to us about them. We spent an hour and a half talking to him about the greatest book of all time.

I challenged him to consider just 10 of the authors—all from one walk of life, one generation, one place, one mood, and one language—and just one controversial subject. Then I asked him: "Would they [the authors] agree?"

He paused and then replied, "No!"

"What would you have?" I said.

Immediately he said, "A conglomeration." I then pointed out to him just some of the many controversial subjects on which biblical authors uniformly agree.

Two days later he committed his life to Christ (the theme of the Bible).

Why all this? Very simple! Any person sincerely seeking truth would at least consider a book with the above unique qualifications.

The above was taken from my book *Evidence That Demands a Verdict*, in which a great deal more information is available on the uniqueness, reliability and validity of the Bible.

• BIBLE STUDY IS WORK

Studying the Word of God is much like walking in the Spirit. It is a steady, day-by-day growth. There are high points and valleys, yet consistency is what pays off.

So often we come to the Word and expect great truths to leap out at us. In our fast-paced society, we want the results the day before yesterday. But God doesn't work that way. He's committed to the process as well as the product. For He knows the one guarantees the other. That is always His way. He took 40 years to prepare Moses, three years for

Paul, and at least 15 for Joseph. Even Christ was prepared for His work.

Bible study is study. Yet so are mathematics, biochemistry, playing the piano, being an expert in video games, being the best plumber, or becoming an airplane pilot. We all study in some way. Some of us study the T.V. We are experts on the shows. The question is: What shall we study? And how?

● THE GOAL

The goal of Bible study is not interpretation but, rather, application. Our target is to have our daily life and ministry become more conformed to the image of Jesus Christ. It is not so much to *know* something but *to do something with what we know.* That is why application, not interpretation, is the goal of Bible study.

Accomplishing this goal depends on three things: First is directing your will. Do you want to study the Word and grow as a Christian, to become conformed to the lifestyle of Christ? Matthew 5:6 says, "Blessed are those who hunger and thirst for righteousness, for they shall be satisfied." But the hunger must be there, the desire must be there. Most of you are reading this book, I hope, because you really desire to know the Word of God.

The second essential ingredient is walking in the Spirit (Ephesians 5:18-19). I call it "logging time" in the Spirit.

Unless you are open to the Holy Spirit, it will be difficult for Him to teach you. The Lord uses clean vessels. We all need to apply 1 John 1:9, "If we confess our sins, He is faithful and righteous to forgive us our sins and to cleanse us from all unrighteousness." Confess any known sin. Make sure each area of your life is yielded to the Holy Spirit (Romans 12:1). Then ask the Holy Spirit to fill you (control and empower you) day-by-day. (To learn more about walking in the Spirit, consult Transferable Concepts numbers 2-4, published by Campus Crusade for Christ, or *He That Is Spiritual*, by Lewis Sperry Chafer. Both should be available in your local Christian book store.)

A FASCINATING BOOK

The third necessity is living in the Word. In other words, "logging time" in the Word. That causes you to become more conformed to the image of Christ both in what you think and in what you do. If you don't spend time in the Word, you may find yourself to be like the people to whom the author of Hebrews wrote:

> "Concerning him we have much to say, and it is hard to explain, since you have become dull of hearing. For though by this time you ought to be teachers, you have need again for someone to teach you the elementary principles of the oracles of God, and you have come to need milk and not solid food. For everyone who partakes only of milk is not accustomed to the word of righteousness, for he is a babe. But solid food is for the mature, who because of practice have their senses trained to discern good and evil" (5:11-14).

And then it is interesting to look at Ephesians 5:18-19 and Colossians 3:16 and compare the results of being *filled* with the Spirit to the results of being *filled* with the Word. You have the same list in both cases, except that when you are filled with the Word, there are two additional elements, teaching and admonishing.

If you are Spirit-filled and you don't know the Word, it is pretty hard to teach. The Holy Spirit brings you to the Word, teaches you the Word, and then carries it out through your life. Claim by faith the teaching ministry of the Holy Spirit (John 14:16-17, 26; 16:13:15; Romans 8:14, 16; 1 Corinthians 2:13). This is so very important.

Donald Grey Barnhouse, the great former pastor of the Tenth Presbyterian Church in Philadelphia, was once traveling on a train and studying his Bible. A young student seated across from him was soaking up all the contemporary news he could by reading a number of popular news magazines. He recognized Dr. Barnhouse, and after some time of traveling he asked, "Dr. Barnhouse, how can I be a man of the Word like you? How can I know the Bible like you?"

Dr. Barnhouse, in his characteristically straightforward manner, replied, "Son, as long as you continue to read those magazines more than you read this Book, you will know more about those magazines than you do about this Book."

Dr. Barnhouse was not saying that knowing our culture is not important. Rather, he was talking of priorities. We always do what we believe to be the most important at the time, no matter what we may say to the contrary.

Oh, how we need to get into the Bible for ourselves! One of the great problems of Christianity today is that we are conditioned to be taught from the Scriptures but *not* to dig out the many truths for ourselves. The process of finding things out for yourself leads to greater personal convictions. It was this attitude that motivated Martin Luther in the 16th century to translate the Scriptures into German, the language of his people, so they could study the Word of God for themselves. This attitude motivated Cameron Townsend to start the work of Wycliffe Bible Translators. It was this God-given desire to have people personally involved in studying God's Word in their own language that made Chet Bitterman, a Wycliffe Bible Translator, willing to give his life recently as a martyr.

● THE PURPOSE AND RESULTS

The Bible makes many bold claims about why it is *the* book to study, to understand, to be at home in, and with which to be intimately acquainted.

The most important reason, and the one that gives meaning to all the others, is that the Bible is the Word of God. How often it is said that the Bible is God's love letter to the world—and how true it is. Because it is the Word of God, its character takes on that of the living God. From its pages come love, justice, mercy, grace and judgment. Wisdom is to be found here. In fact, help in every aspect of life is promised: guidance for every need; peace for every troubled soul. Paul exhorted Timothy: "All Scripture is inspired by God and profitable for teaching, for reproof, for correction, for training in righteousness; that the man of God may be adequate, equipped for every good work" (2 Timothy 3:16-17).

The Word of God is powerful and lasting. Jesus said, "Heaven and earth will pass away, but My words shall not pass away" (Matthew 24:35). The prophet Isaiah said: "The grass withers, the flower fades, but the word of our God stands forever" (40:8). David in Psalms 19 and 119 made bold claims for the power of God's Word. It heals, rejoices, enlightens, offers wisdom, and guides in purity.

Men and women of God have always been men and women of the Word. Ezra made it his passion. David, his meditation. Joshua, his way. Make no mistake, the Bible changes lives. As we are exposed to His Word, God uses it as a chisel to mold us into the image of His Son.

When you study the Word, it will change your life in many areas. First, your *attitudes* will begin to change. For example, as you get into the Word, you understand that your spiritual victories come from the Lord. Thus, they don't lead to pride because you give God the glory (1 Corinthians 15:10). Also, as you get into the Word, you start to look at your problems from God's viewpoint—more as opportunities than as problems (2 Corinthians 12:10; Philippians 4:6: 1 Thessalonians 5:18; Hebrews 12:5-11; James 1:2, 3).

Your attitude toward pride starts to change. Some people get to thinking that after they help lead someone to Christ, God is pretty fortunate to have them on His team. Philippians 2:3, however, speaks of how the study of the Word will affect pride.

As Bible study changes your attitudes, the eventual result will be the *transformation of your life.* Paul said in Romans 12:2a, "Do not be conformed to this world, but be transformed by the renewing of your mind."

KNOW YOUR BIBLE

As God transforms your mind you will begin to think like Christ. Paul said, "We are destroying speculations and every lofty thing raised up against the knowledge of God" (2 Corinthians 10:5a). Wow! Paul should be on a university campus today! He went on to say, "And we are taking every thought captive to the obedience of Christ" (2 Corinthians 10:5b).

As we take our thoughts captive to the obedience of Christ, we start thinking like Christ. Then what happens to our actions? We start to act like Christ: "For as he thinks within himself, so he is" (Proverbs 23:7a). This is so important in our culture. When you are confronted with difficult situations and temptations, if you are thinking like Christ and you know God's Word, your actions are going to be Christ-like.

Another result of Bible study is *security* along with *confidence*. A secure, stable man can endure many things in life. In Ephesians, Paul showed his awareness of our need to be secure in discussing those spiritual gifts that relate to ministering the Word of God: "For the equipping of the saints for the work of service, to the building up of the body of Christ; until we all attain to the unity of the faith, and of the knowledge of the Son of God, to a mature man, to the measure of the stature which belongs to the fulness of Christ" (Ephesians 4:12, 13).

If you have strength, security and confidence in each area of your life, what do you have? Maturity. That is the essence of Hebrews 5:14: "But solid food is for the mature, who because of practice have their senses trained to discern good and evil."

So, Bible study changes your personal attitudes, transforms your mind and life, and gives you confidence and security. The result of all that is maturity.

Your message and your witness will also be affected by studying the Scriptures. Bible study reveals biblical life principles that you need to incorporate into your witness and messages. More and more, I am trying to take my illustrations from the Word of God when I speak. That way, the people will be learning the Bible as well as getting a biblical principle from it.

Today, we need to communicate God's truth about man, about history, about life. I just love to go into a university classroom and speak about God's perspective on history, sex, war, hatred, prejudices, and any other topic. The students don't know what to say. Most of them have not known prior to that point that the Bible even spoke to such issues.

The Bible must be incorporated into your witness because the spiritual battlefield is the minds of men and women. When you look at today's literature, listen to the speakers, and see what is happening in our culture, you realize that everyone is trying to get to the will of man through his mind and his emotions, especially through the media. Films, television and magazines are all attempting to have us believe people need to buy certain products and, more important, live a certain way. Given all the philosophies that compete today for the allegiance of men and women, the only way in which we can really capture a person's mind is by the grace of God. We explain the Word of God to people, live it out before them, and then let the Holy Spirit convict and enlighten them.

I do not believe a political philosophy will ultimately capture the minds of men. But as you explain the Word of God to them, you are going to see lives changed.

●　　THE PLAN

This book is structured somewhat differently from most other books on Bible study methods. You learn, in a simple, quick, yet effective way (1) how to study the Bible and (2) how to apply the Word to bring about significant changes in your life. You might look at it this way: The goal is not so much to master the Word, but to have the Word master you. The difference is one of focus and attitude.

KNOW YOUR BIBLE

You will not learn a great variety of Bible study methods in this book. Instead, you will learn one method that you can use profitably for the rest of your life. Usually, when you take a "How to Study the Bible" course, the teacher will give you four to seven methods, and you never seem to learn any one very well. I have seen people take Bible study courses, and afterward I say to them, "How was it?"

They say, "Great. I have some fantastic notes."

"Are you using them?" I ask.

"Well, no. It is pretty difficult," is the common answer.

My desire is that you will not say that when you have finished this book and put its principles into daily practice.

We are going to look at one method, and we are going to learn it inside and out. You are going to know it better than you know your best friend. If you apply this approach, you will never again open the Bible and read its pages and not learn something. You will begin to see things in familiar passages that you never knew existed there. You will be talking to your wife or girl friend about love, and all of a sudden, as the fruit of your Bible study, you will remember what you learned about biblical love. It will be natural to apply what you have learned in all types of situations throughout the day. You will be able to turn a bogged-down or boring group Bible study into an exciting experience.

● WHY A METHOD?

Why do you need a method to study the Bible? It is simply not enough to know what you want to do. You have to know the right way of doing it. If you have a goal but no plan, or method, for achieving it, you will probably fail. But if you have a good method, you can get what you want out of your study.

A good plan is essential in any undertaking. One of the reasons the student radical movement failed in the late '60s and early '70s was that the students had plenty of motivation but no direction and no plan. They had no clear-cut method to help them achieve their goals. They didn't know how to get to where they were trying to go.

And as we come to the study of the Word of God, one of the most important of all undertakings, we need to know how to get to the desired result, conformity to the image of Christ.

The dangers in not approaching Bible study methodically are many and great. For example, there is the danger of not understanding a passage properly because you simply have not observed carefully what it is saying. There is also the danger of misunderstanding because you have only partial information on the subject in question; you have not considered the amplification or clarification offered in other passages of Scripture. And there is the danger of misunderstanding because you have lifted the passage out of context; you have not considered how its meaning is influenced by the verses preceding and following it. These are just some of the dangers.

• PRACTICE, PRACTICE

Your success with the study method presented in this book depends on your willingness to practice. Practice is the means by which excellence in any skill is achieved. When I play racquetball, I must practice consistently in order to do well. Not only must I practice, but I also must know *how* to practice. For example: Hit the ball squarely, follow through, keep my eye on the ball, and so on. And all this must be done at the same time! When I began in racquetball, I couldn't do this all at the same time and still do it well. But as I practiced and learned *what* and *how* to practice, I gained competence and the results were rewarding. (My six year old son Sean was asked, "What is it like when your daddy loses?" And he answered, "I don't know!")

The same is true of Bible study methods. People ask me, "How can I get the quality of results you do?" By practice, I tell them. That is the key. Provided we all have the same Bible, the same Holy Spirit and the same approach to study, the only variables are TIME and EFFORT. No one would expect you to go out tomorrow and play the piano as well as Arthur Rubenstien or tennis as well as John McEnroe. They have practiced and followed a course of action to excel.

Diligent practice is likewise essential in studying God's Word. There is no easy method, if easy means a short cut, little work, or short study. Excellence is not gained at a small cost. Anyone in athletics, public speaking or the arts is acutely aware that excellence comes at a price.

Yet although it is not easy, in one sense Bible study is not difficult, either. There is a balance to be struck. The method I will describe is one that can be applied anywhere or anytime and for any length of time, be it five minutes or five hours. Now, that is easy and simple and encouraging. But in that time, it requires thinking, understanding and application of the method we shall learn. That is the difficult part: making the time to study and persevering.

A methodical Bible study is not an academic course, but a lifetime of study. It is not a formula, but a process you work through. It is not a shortcut, but it is work. And it is not a mold, but an outlet for your personality. It is a simple, organized approach to discovering God's truth.

• WHERE ARE WE GOING?

What are we going to be doing in the next few chapters? We will walk you through the Bible study method step-by-step so that you can see exactly how it works. We'll overview it first, and then we will apply it together. The appendix is full of examples of the various steps to be followed in our method.

We start with one book of the Bible, first taking the big picture and then working down from there. We begin with a wide-angle lens to see the whole and then move in with a microscope to see its parts. When I start tearing a car engine apart, I like to see it put together first. I used to rebuild old cars and then sell them. If I could see a car engine together and then take it apart myself, I could put it back together again. That is what we need to do with the Scriptures—see the whole, go to the parts, and then see their relationship to the whole again.

In Chicago, they have a number of skyscrapers, including some of the tallest buildings in the world. The very tallest of these is the Sears Tower. It is huge. You get to the building, you stand there and look up, and it looks as though it is going to the end of the sky. I like to put my back against the side of a building and then look up. It gives you a greater concept of the size of the building. When I went inside the Sears Tower and looked around, I saw the connector for the heating plant. The connector was not very big—it was only a 75¢ item—but it was the key piece for the entire heating plant of that huge building. Now, if I had just gone inside, without seeing the outside of the building, and looked at that little connector, I could have said, "So what? A motorcycle has a bigger one than that." But after seeing the size of the building and then looking at that minute part—wow, that little thing helps run the whole building! In other words, the part took on significant meaning *only* in light of the whole.

What we are going to do in our Bible study is start with a book, then go to the individual chapters, then to the paragraphs, the verses, the phrases, and finally to the words—all in the context of that whole book. The book that will serve as an example for our study is the Gospel of John, especially chapters three and four. Although we will refer to many other scriptural examples as we develop our method, our repeated use of John 3 and 4 will give us continuity. Also, John is easy to learn from. I think he had Bible study method students in mind when he wrote.

We will start with the big picture and work down to the details, through several logical steps. We begin with a book chart for the book we have chosen and develop chapter titles. That enables us to see the entire book outlined and pictured by chapters. When we go to the paragraphs, we develop paragraph titles. After that we look at the verses and the individual words.

Then we begin the steps of observation. Observation asks, "What does it say?" Or you might say, "What do I see?" Instead of always using the term "observation," we're going to interchange it with the phrase "*See it!*" I think that really communicates the idea involved in this step. *To see* what is there is our goal.

How much you see is important. We will learn how to see. You say, "How to see?" That's right. You need to train yourself in what to look for.

How much you see usually will determine your interpretation, which is the next step. It asks, "What does it mean?" Then again, rather than always using the term "interpretation," we will interchange it with the phrase "Know it!" Here we want to understand what is being said.

Following interpretation is application, the goal of Bible study. Here we ask, "What does it mean to me?" or "How does it apply to me?" From a biblical perspective, to know and not do is not to know at all. That is the whole point of James 2:14-26. To signify application, we will use the phrase "Do it!"

These, then, are the three general steps in our Bible study method:

1. See it (observation).
2. Know it (interpretation).
3. Do it (application).

Assignment

1. Read Psalm 19:7-11 and write down three reasons studying God's Word is good for you personally.
2. Read John 9 three times at one sitting.

▼ STEP TWO ▼

Charting

▼ CHAPTER TWO ▼

Let's Get
the Big Picture

Have you heard that old expression, "he can't see the forest for the trees"? It means, of course, that a person is so immersed in the details that he cannot see the whole picture of what he is doing.

The whole gives meaning and understanding to the parts. For example, what if we were in London and I said, "Meet me at Big Ben in two hours." And suppose you did not have a clue about what Big Ben was or where Big Ben was located. You could spend all day looking for it. However, if I told you it was a famous building with a clock and gave you a map—presto! You would know precisely where to go. The map is the whole. It gives meaning to the parts, namely, places in London like Big Ben, the Houses of Parliament, Soho, and Piccadilly Circus.

Consider another illustration. The coach yells "chalk talk" for tomorrow morning at eight. The husky football players amble in, and the coach goes to the blackboard to explain their assignments for a certain play. The coach is charting his plays. He gives the team the "big picture," a whole view. But what if the coach went up to the blackboard and drew only one circle on the board for the right tackle, then explained his blocking assignments with no other men symbolized on the board! It wouldn't mean a thing. The tackle's job has meaning only in light of the whole, the entire team.

LET'S GET THE BIG PICTURE

The same principle holds true with a military general planning his battle strategy. The small skirmishes have meaning only in light of the whole battle plan.

The picture that we attempt to get through doing charts is only the beginning of the important whole-to-parts process. We start by getting an overall picture of a book. Then we take the book apart for all the details we can find. And that gives us a greater appreciation of the whole. We check our detailed findings against the original big picture we had in the beginning, to see if we were correct. We note whether there are any changes that need to be made. The process is whole-to-parts-to-whole development.

•   THE BOOK CHART

You have had a hard day and are getting ready for an early trip to bed when the phone rings. You answer and hear the greeting of your daughter who is away at college. After the opening formalities, she says, "Dad, my friend is talking to one of the guys at school about spiritual things, and he is having a tough time understanding the resurrection of Jesus. Can you give me some Scripture passages that she can go through with him?"

How many passages could you recall at that instant so that she could write them down and give them to her friend? If you have to answer "Few" or "None," you are going to find the book chart extremely useful in the future.

What exactly is the value of a book chart? The book chart will help you recall what is in a given chapter of a book of the Bible, because through your study of it you will be able to fix it in your mind without special effort.

First, by using a book chart, you can see a whole book at a glance.
Second, it reveals the overall theme of the book.
Third, it gives a biblical "clothes line" on which to hang specific passages and verses. When you are hanging your clothes out to dry in the sun, you hang them on a

clothesline. But suppose you do not have a clothesline. You cannot hang your clothes on a sky hook. So often, we pull verses out of the Bible and have no idea where they fit in. Since we have no idea what to do with them, we just write them off. Using our first illustration, you could also see the chart as the forest where you put the individual trees, the verses.

Fourth, the chart makes a book easy to remember, and a lot easier to teach.

Before you get started on the book chart, however, let me remind you that since the Bible is the Word of God, you should always begin your study by asking the Lord for guidance and insight. Your attitude must be, "Open my eyes that I may behold wonderful things from Thy Word and be willing to apply them."

• READ

After talking to the Lord comes reading His Word. Then comes more reading, and finally reading it again. There is no short cut to reading. There is no better way to get accustomed to a book than to read it at least three or four times. G. Campbell Morgan, the great biblical expository, would read a book 30 times before he attempted to study it. It is especially important to read a book through in one sitting.

The first time you read a book, look for a stated purpose. In John it says, "These things have been written that you may believe that Jesus is the Christ" (John 20:31a). So, what is the purpose of John? "That you may believe that Jesus is the Christ."

During the second reading, look for *repeated phrases*. For example, Matthew kept saying, "When Jesus had finished," Genesis often says, "These are the generations of..." Looking for repeated phrases will help you understand the development of the purpose of the book. There are chronological divisions such as in the book of Exodus; geographical divisions such as in the book of 1 and 2 Kings.

LET'S GET THE BIG PICTURE

Now, let's break those divisions down to manageable units. For the sake of clarity, we will drop titles like geographical and biographical. Instead, use words like "places" and "persons." They communicate! Here is what we mean: Books in Scripture are *all* structured around five principle areas.

1. Persons (1 and 2 Samuel, 1 and 2 Kings, Genesis 2-50)
2. Places (Acts, Joshua)
3. Events (the gospels, Genesis 1-11)
4. Ideas (Romans, Proverbs)
5. Time (Luke, Revelation)

These are things to look for as you read a book.

Chapter Titles

A book chart contains chapter titles for each chapter. Developing those involves finding a title that best describes all the paragraphs in a chapter and relates them to the theme of the chapter. You might say, "Well, that's easy." No, it isn't. To do it right, so that it is effective for you, takes practice. But once you get it down, it becomes easier and easier, just like playing racquetball! For our study, the title needs to describe the content of that chapter (you can do a book chart by using titles that reflect the theology, the meaning, etc., of the chapter).

One point must be noted. As you give titles to the chapters, remember that the chapter divisions in the Bible are not inspired, nor are the paragraph or verse divisions. For the most part, they serve as natural breaks, but some are in unfortunate places. So, in your study, as you gain knowledge of the content of the chapter, you may want to include some verses of one chapter under the heading of another chapter, or even make your own paragraph divisions. Actually, each chapter could be looked at as one man's way of dividing Scripture into segments. Looking at it this way should help you to feel freer to change some chapter divisions when that would lead to better understanding.

▼ STEP TWO ▼
KNOW YOUR BIBLE

Simply use a sheet of paper (I prefer an 8 1/2 x 11 size) turned sideways to construct the chart. The number of columns will vary with the number of chapters in the book. In other words, the Gospel of John has 21 chapters, so you would use both sides of the paper to make 21 columns. Each book of the Bible can be put on one sheet of paper using front and back.

Book Chart

_____

Chapters	1	2	3	4	5	6	7
Chapter Titles							

(See pages 140-148 for further samples.)

As noted earlier, titles can reflect either the meaning (theology) or the basic content.

For our study, we will develop a book chart with titles reflecting content. (If you want to learn the Bible, be sure to think through and come up with your own chapter titles, even if the publisher of your Bible may have provided some already.) Therefore, each of your chapter titles will recall to your mind the content of that chapter. If I wanted to do a theological book chart, the titles would recall the theology of that chapter. Whatever your purpose is, the chapter titles bring it to mind.

Often the titles describing content are those done first, since the correct meaning follows from how well you observe the content. You can see this by examining different possible titles for John 11. One possible title of _content_ for the chapter might be "The Resurrection of Lazarus," while one possible title of _meaning_ might be "Christ's Power Over Death."

Your title should not be so general that it might fit any chapter of the book you are studying. When I recall specific titles, I know right where they go. Look at your titles as *handles* with which to grasp the content of that chapter.

Keep the titles *short* so they are easy to remember. If you keep your titles as brief and yet as comprehensive as possible, it will help you recall where certain biblical truths are found. Be careful to avoid details.

Don't hesitate to put a little *humor* in your titles—it is a great way to recall a chapter. For example, several students in one of my classes were very creative. One titled John 4 "Well, Well." She was emphasizing the woman at the *well* and the nobleman's son made *well*. Another student titled John 9 "The Blind Man Sees More Than the Pharisees." He was emphasizing that the Pharisees, with all their theological training, did not have the spiritual insight of the blind man. So when you make your titles, be creative! Creative titles will help you later remember the content of the chapter.

Let me close this section with a couple of examples of the benefits of creating book charts with good, specific chapter titles. First, a lot of times when I go to bed at night, I go through a book of the Bible in my mind by going through my book chart. And second, I remember one time when I was traveling from Boston to Texas. I had just begun to date Dottie (now my wife). My father-in-law-to-be was driving Dottie back to Texas, and I rode down as far as Washington, D.C., with them. At one point I suggested, "Let's study the Bible." My future father-in-law was driving, and I said, "Stop, let me drive, and I'll teach the book of Romans." Then, without any Bible or notes, I taught the entire book of Romans by recalling the book chart I had memorized. It astounded my future father-in-law. I do not tell this story to brag, but to show you how you, too, can plant the Word of God in your mind and heart by developing book charts.

Assignment

1. Read John 1-6 three times.
2. On an 8 1/2 x 11 piece of paper, write chapter titles on a chart for John 1-3 only. (See Appendix pp. 140-144 for examples.) Give a title to each chapter.

Paragraph Titles

Now that you have the chapters titled, you are ready to move on to the next step in getting to know the content of the book you are studying. Look at the individual paragraphs within a chapter and assign titles to them. These titles go in the column underneath the chapter title. Each chapter should be divided into a number of sections, equaling the number of paragraphs in that chapter.

To do this, you obviously need a Bible that indicates paragraphing. I like to use the paragraph divisions given in *The New American Standard Bible* (NASB), and I will be using them in this book. (Example below.) That translation indicates the beginning of new paragraphs by putting the number of the first verse in boldface.

22 ªJohn 2:2 ᵇLuke 24:8; John 2:17; 12:16; 14:26 ᶜPs. 16:10; Luke 24:26f.; John 20:9; Acts 13:33

Scripture, and the word which Jesus had spoken.
23 Now when He was in Jerusalem at ªthe Passover, during the feast, many believed in His name, ᵇbeholding His signs which He was doing.

23 ªJohn 2:13 ᵇJohn 2:11

24 But Jesus, on His part, was not entrusting Himself to them, for ªHe knew all men,

24 ªActs 1:24; 15:8

25 and because He did not need anyone to bear witness concerning man ªfor He Himself knew what was in man.

You can, however, use whatever translation you prefer, as long as it provides paragraph divisions. But be aware of the fact that not all translations break chapters into the exact same paragraphs. That is no problem. As with chapters, you can, on occasion, feel free to make your own paragraph divisions if you don't agree with the ones in your Bible.

LET'S GET THE BIG PICTURE

Book Chart on John

Ch. 1	Ch. 2	Ch. 3	Ch. 4	Ch. 5	Ch. 6
Jesus Recognized					
:1-5 Recognized as the *Word*					
:6-8 Recognized by *John*					
:9-13 Recognized by *us*					
:14-18 Recognized by His *glory*					
:19-28 Recognized by *religious leaders*					
:29-34 Recognized as *Lamb of God*					
:35-42 Recognized by *Andrew*					
:43-51 Recognized by *Nathaniel*					

Your titles will vary according to your knowledge of the Scriptures—more specifically, to your knowledge of that book. (Your individual, unique way of expressing your thoughts will also come through.) If you don't have a lot of knowledge, your titles might be a little more detailed. If you have studied a book, they might be more general. Since I have studied John a lot, my titles will be a little different from those of some other people.

KNOW YOUR BIBLE

Let's consider John 1 so you can get an idea of how to do it. You can also look at the accompanying chart, which has the same information I will be discussing. The chapter title I have for John 1 is "Jesus Recognized." For somebody new to Bible study, who is just starting the book of John, it might not be a good one. But it is a good one for me. Let me show you what I mean. The first paragraph of John 1 includes verses 1-5. For that paragraph I have "Recognized as the Word." For verses 6-8 I have "Recognized by John," because John the Baptist recognized Jesus. For verses 9-13 I have "Recognized by us," meaning the world. For verses 14-18 I have "Recognized by His glory." For verses 19-28 I have "Recognized by religious leaders." For verses 29-34 I have "Recognized as Lamb of God." For verses 35-42 it is "Recognized by Andrew." And finally, for verses 43-51, I have "Recognized by Nathaniel." It all ties together with the chapter title: "Jesus Recognized."

Once you have done that you can recall all the content of John 1. "Recognized" is the key word here. He was recognized by John, recognized by us, recognized by His glory, and so on. This title recalls for me the basic content of each paragraph. From your background, the titles might not recall the basic content of John 1. You create titles that are helpful *for you*, not someone else. The more you can relate the paragraph titles to the chapter title, the easier it is to recall the chapter content later.

Some people prefer to come up with a chapter title *after* studying each paragraph. Then they come up with the paragraph titles. Others prefer to develop the paragraph titles first and then find an appropriate chapter title. Which is best? Neither. Do what you find easiest and most helpful. I personally do the chapter title first.

Make your titles, both chapter and paragraph, as brief as possible. The fewer words the better. To recall the content of John 2, I have the chapter title "Wedding Wine and Temple Cleansed." First, we have the wedding in Cana, where the water was turned into wine; and then we have the temple being cleansed by Jesus. Chapter 3 is "Born Again Through Believing In Christ."

Let me digress for a moment and show you why I have that title for John 3. The first paragraph talks about being born again. How are you born again? It is through believing—second paragraph. Then, the last part of the chapter emphasizes believing in Jesus rather than John the Baptist. John the Baptist points out that he must decrease and Jesus must increase. And there I've got a handle to recall John 3—"Born Again Through Believing In Christ."

After you have completed both chapter titles and paragraph titles, you will find it very beneficial to record other helpful information on the book chart.

First, at the bottom of each vertical chapter column, section off an area in which to indicate the key word and key verse of that chapter.

And second, in some unused space of your chart, indicate the following for the entire book you are studying: author, date, place, key verse, key word, historical setting, geographical setting. Include any pertinent information concerning the book you are studying. A Bible handbook, a commentary, a dictionary, or a study Bible will have this information.

Assignment

1. Read John 1-3 again.
2. Add paragraph titles to your book chart for John 1-3.

• SUMMARY

Let's review. Our first emphasis is on reading. The more times we can read a passage or a book, the better.

Next is the book chart. There we take a book, or a large section of a book, such as John 1-6, and put titles down that correctly summarize each chapter and paragraph. The titles should be as brief as possible and looked at as a *handle* to recall the content of that section.

▼ STEP TWO ▼
KNOW YOUR BIBLE

Assignment

1. Read John 8.
2. Construct a book chart for John 8 with both chapter and paragraph titles.

▼ STEP THREE ▼

Observation "See It"

▼ *CHAPTER THREE* ▼

Know What to Look For

Early in my ministry with Campus Crusade for Christ, I was assigned to Argentina. When I got there, I discovered that their favorite sport is not American football or basketball but soccer. And the first time I watched a soccer game, I did not understand it at all. I had no idea of what was supposed to happen on the field.

But after I learned the rules, the plays, and how teams operate, I knew what to look for. Then I saw a great deal more of the complex plays as they developed, and my enjoyment of the game increased tremendously.

The same is true when you study the Bible. If you don't know what to look for, you are not going to find much of interest. The Bible will simply be something to read and something from which you can pick up occasional inspiration.

When you learn what to look for, however, you will suddenly begin to see the marvelous facets of God's revelation to us. To see how the Bible unfolds the truth of God, you need to develop an approach to observation that will let you, with the help of the Holy Spirit, understand what God is really doing.

Let me illustrate. The FBI has training films that are used to teach agents the "art of observation." There is one three-minute film that comes with a list of over 100 questions on what you should have observed from seeing the film for the first time. Of the film, which shows a quick robbery, questions are asked such as, "Was the man left-handed?" "What was in his back pocket?" "Did the lady wear a watch?" And so on. I know of a professor who shows this film to his Bible study methods class in seminary, and the average score is 35 out of over 100 questions. Yet one year, an ex-FBI agent was in his class, and he had never seen that particular training film before. But he got every answer correct. He knew what to look for. That is the key.

Besides not knowing what to look for, most people do not see much more because they do not know how to look. It is like witnessing. If you do not know how to witness, you usually do not witness. If you do not know how to study the Bible, or how to look, you do not take the trouble to look. This is true of any subject. Take art or music, for example. Some people will pass by a great painting and make a glib comment, while another group of people will come by and rave about it. What is the difference? The latter know how to look and what to look for. They know what makes a painting exciting, such as movement, form, gesture—important things about it. This is why it is often said of those who criticize great works of art that the painting is really judging them, rather than they the painting. The same is true of those who comment that they study the Bible but cannot find that much to get out of it. Their comment actually says more about them than about the Bible.

Another reason people see very little when they study the Bible is that they fail to look. You know everybody has one thing in common—time. But the thing that seems to be manifested differently in people is effort. Some people put forth a lot more effort than others. As I have said before, there is no easy method, no special short cut. Biblical elbow grease is essential. But the rewards are deeply satisfying—knowledge of God, knowledge of His word, and a changed life.

• THE SIX BIGGIES

To play baseball, we need to have a bat. To play the piano, we must have the music. To construct a building, the right tools, equipment and blueprints are needed. We also need the right tools to study the Bible.

41

KNOW YOUR BIBLE

In observation, the right tools will enable you not only to see things in the Word that you have not seen before, but they will also enable you to see the *right* things. Why can the U.S. Secret Service agents spot a forged one dollar bill faster than anyone? Because they know what to look for. They have been trained in observation.

In Bible study, we learn what to look for by asking the right questions. There are key questions you must ask of the passage you are studying. The first questions are so simple that they could insult one's intelligence. Let me go down through them. They are Who? What? When? Where? Why? How? You say, "Just a minute, Josh. We got these in the third grade!" That's right. This is third grade material. But some of the things we got in the third grade were great! The problem is that we forgot them by the time we entered the fourth grade.

You might call these six words *surfacers*, for they bring to our attention, or to the surface, what is in a passage. They help us know what to look for. It is as if we put all of Scripture in six different flour sifters, and as we shake them, the "what" sifter reveals what is specifically happening in each passage. The "who" sifter brings to the surface the personalities; the "where" sifter, the places, and so on. Applying the steps of observation gives us a legitimate basis to be "snoopy." All of us at one time or another have the urge to be snoopy. Now *you* can be super snoopy. A great compliment would be God's saying to a believer, "You sure have been snoopy when it comes to my Word!"

Now, as you ask yourself these questions, what will you do with your answers? You place them in an observation chart — the next step after the book charts we looked at in the preceding chapter.

What does an observation chart look like? It is composed of three columns. Look at the sample blank chart below. Notice in the left-hand column that you record the Scripture reference being observed. In the center column you write down any observations you make. In the right-hand column are questions of interpretation, or interpretive questions. I have learned over the years that if I do not write down a question immediately when it comes to my mind, I quickly forget it. As you make observa-

OBSERVATION CHART

Scripture	Observations	Interpretive Questions

(See pages 149-162 for samples.)

tions of a passage, many questions will surface. Write them down immediately in the "Interpretive Questions" column of the observation chart.

As you begin your observation, you first ask "*Who?*" Who are the personalities in the passage you are studying? Who did it? Who can do it? Who is it talking about?

The second question is "*What?*" As soon as you ask "What?" you can go on forever. What is he saying? What is he talking about? What is happening? What did they do? What caused that? The list of possible "what" questions is endless.

In answering the "what" question, also consider the atmosphere of the passage. Was Paul exhorting? Was Jesus instructing? Were there feelings involved?

The atmosphere of a passage is understood best by putting yourself back into the situation of the author. Was it joyful? Was it depressing? How did the circumstances affect his attitude? If you were the blind man in John 9, blind from birth, how would you feel if Christ healed you? If you were Abraham, would the pain of the raised knife against your promised son, Isaac, pierce your heart?

When I studied the leper in Mark 1:40-44, I put myself in the same position on the floor as he would have been in while begging of Christ. All of a sudden, I realized probably the last thing a leper would expect is for anyone to touch him. You couldn't ask anyone to have to reach down and touch that dirty, diseased, rotten skin. And yet that's just what Christ did. It immediately went through my mind, *He touched me! He Cares! He really does! He cares!* And the leper was healed. I knew that if Christ had not touched him, had not *cared*, that man would never have been healed!

Next ask "*When?*" When did it happen? When will it happen? When can it happen? And as you start asking the passage this question, the time element starts jumping out. But if you do not ask "when" some important things can escape you. So ask "When?"

Next is "*Where?*" Where is he going? Where did it happen? Where will it take place? Ask the passage "Where?" as many times as you usefully can.

Then ask "*Why?*" Why did he say that? Why did he do that? Why did he go there? Again, you could just go on and on asking, "Why?"

Finally, ask "*How?*" How did it happen? How can it happen? How involves the process. How was Christ crucified? Is that important? How was the wall of Jerusalem built in Nehemiah's day? That information is critical to understanding his book.

There are several approaches to asking the six questions. Some ask "Who?" of all the verses they are studying before they go on to the other questions, recording observations and interpretive questions. Others prefer to ask all the questions of each verse before proceeding to the next verse. The choice is up to you. I generally prefer asking each question of all the verses before going on to the next question.

Going back now to our observation chart, in the left hand column for Scripture, you can do one of two things. You can put down the reference, where the verse is found, or you can write it out. If you are doing this chart with just one verse, I would write the verse out there so you can look directly at it and make observations without going to the Bible. Do whatever is most beneficial for you.

The center column is where you write out your observations — that is, anything you have observed as a result of asking the six major questions of the passage.

Sometimes you will be observing something and suddenly, out of nowhere, a question will come up, a question for which you do not have any answer. That question immediately goes in the right-hand column. You should never write a question in the observation column. Questions always go in the column for interpretive questions. This helps you think clearly when you go on to the steps of interpretation. If you do not write the questions down, you are going to forget them. Later in the step of interpretation, you simply answer those that are most pertinent to understanding the passage or subject you are studying, or those that time permits. But every time you follow through with one question, you will know the answer the next time you come to that same question. Look at the accompanying partial observation chart for John 1:1-5 to see how the three parts of the chart look when filled out.

OBSERVATION CHART

John 1:15

Student Sample

Scripture	Observations	Interpretive Questions
"In the beginning was the Word, and the Word was with God, and the Word was God. He was in the beginning with God. All things came into being through Him; and apart from Him nothing came into being that has come into being. In Him was life; and the life was the light of men. And the light shines in the darkness; and the darkness did not comprehend it."	WHO: The Word, God, He, the light, the life, Him, men WHAT: John is describing: The Word was in the beginning The word was with God The Word was God He was in the beginning All things came into being through Him In Him (Jesus) is the light – shines on men Darkness doesn't overpower the light The life was the light of men WHEN: Creation or the creative process has already taken place. Nothing came into being that *has* in the Beginning was the Word WHERE: The Word was with God He was in the beginning with God WHY: HOW: Creation came about by an infinite, eternal God creating.	Who is the Word? Is it Jesus? Who is the Life? Who does "the men" refer to? (All men, certain men, etc.) What does "Word" mean? What does "darkness" refer to? What does it mean "the life *was* the light of men"? What kind of "life" does this mean? (eternal, abundant, etc.) When was "the life" the light of men? (always, period of time) Why does John call Jesus the "Word"? Why does John contain John 1:1–5 in his gospel account? (heresy, etc.) Why does it say "the darkness *did not* overcome" (Is the battle over with)? How does the "light" shine? (through creation, men, etc.)

KNOW WHAT TO LOOK FOR

Let's look at John 3 as an example of how to develop the six questions. Start with verse 1. "There was a man of the Pharisees, named Nicodemus, a ruler of the Jews." We'll start with "who." In the center column, I usually write "who," and I box the word in or underline it to highlight it and I write it bold enough so that it jumps right out. That way I know I am dealing with "who."

Turn to John 3:1 now and take a few minutes to see how many observations you can make by simply asking the question "Who?" Then come back and let's compare.

Isn't it amazing what you can discover just by asking questions! You probably saw some things you have never seen before about John 3:1 by just asking the question "Who?" What are some "who" observations of John 3:1? Well, he was a *man*, he was a *Pharisee*, his name was *Nicodemus*, he was a *ruler*, and he was a *Jew*. All in verse 1. (Verse 10 tells us he was also a teacher.)

Now, what questions would come out of these observations? What was a Pharisee? How did a man become a Pharisee? Who was a Pharisee? What did a Pharisee do? What was the relationship of a Pharisee to a ruler? Did he have to be a ruler to be a Pharisee? What were the qualifications to be a Pharisee? What education was necessary? Write down all these questions. What other questions would you have? What is a Jew? What is a ruler? You could think of many such questions.

You will notice that there are other observations to make and record in the observation column: a Pharisee holds a religious office; a teacher is in an educational position; a ruler is a political figure. In addition, Nicodemus, being a Jew, was a member of a minority race which at that time was subject to the rule of the Roman Empire.

Jumping ahead a little, consider how you might apply these simple observations in witnessing. You are talking to a religious leader. What do you do? You say, "Let me show you what Jesus said to a religious leader." You go back to Nicodemus in John 3.

Or suppose you are talking to a political leader and you want to witness to him. You remember that Nicodemus was a political leader, so you show this man what Jesus said to Nicodemus.

Or you are in a discussion with someone from a minority race. You might say "You know Jesus talked to a man from a minority race. Notice what he said to him..." You go back to Nicodemus in John 3 and explain their conversation. John 3:1-10 is also one of the main passages I use when addressing an educational group. I say, "Let me show you what Jesus said to an educator..."

You could write down many interpretive questions about Nicodemus. What is the significance of the name "Nicodemus"? What did it mean? All these questions come by asking "Who?"

"When?" There is nothing significant in verse 1 in answer to the question "When?" Many times you will not find an answer to every question in a certain verse or passage. But if you do not ask, you may miss something that is there.

So you move ahead and ask "When?" of verse 2. "This man came to Him by night, and said to Him, 'Rabbi, we know that You have come from God as a teacher; for no one can do these signs that You do unless God is with him'" (John 3:2). Any indication there of time? If there is, write it in the observation column of the chart. And we do have the phrase "came to Him by night." What observation could you make from the fact that Nicodemus came "by night"?

Let's consider some reasons he might have come at night. What I do is indent the "Why?"—since we are under "When?"— "Why at night?" A little imagination is needed here. You need to try to put yourself in the same situation, or in that other person's shoes, and ask yourself why *you* would come at night. Then write down your observations. After you have exhausted your observations, you develop some questions. Later, as you go through the steps of interpretation and answer your questions, you will begin to see which answers, if any, are correct. At this point you are just immersing yourself in the passage.

▼ STEP THREE ▼
KNOW WHAT TO LOOK FOR

Suppose you were a Jew, a Pharisee, a ruler and a teacher, and someone like Jesus came to town. Why would you go to Him at night? Let's list the possible reasons here under steps of observation.

The first possibility is that he did not want anyone to see him. Why would he not want anyone to see him? Perhaps it was fear of the Pharisees, the Jews, the teachers, or the rulers. Why else would he not want to be seen going to Jesus? Pride is a possibility. What if you were *the* teacher of Israel? You might be afraid to be seen in the presence of Christ because of professional or peer pressure. The same could be true in regard to the Jews, the Pharisees, or the rulers.

Why else would Nicodemus come at night? He could have been too busy in the daytime. If you are a Pharisee, a ruler, a Jew and a teacher, your time will be limited during the day for extracurricular activities.

Why else would he come at night? Maybe he wanted to talk to Jesus alone. During the daytime, all the crowds were around Jesus. Therefore, Nicodemus might have waited until night so he could have a very private conversation with Jesus. (If that was the reason, his plan backfired. The whole world has read about it for 2,000 years). Let me summarize our speculative observations in outline form:

Why did Nicodemus come to Jesus at night?

I.   No one to see him
    A. Because of fear
        1. Pharisees
        2. Rulers
        3. Jews
        4. Teachers
    B. Because of pride
        1. Pharisees
        2. Rulers
        3. Jews
        4. Teachers
II. Busy in the daytime
III. Talk to Jesus alone

By now you are starting to understand a little bit more of the passage—in fact, a lot more about the encounter of Nicodemus with Jesus.

Is there any other "When?" in verse 2? "We know that You have come from God." You could write down in the question column, "When did Jesus come from God?" There are a number of observations you could make regarding the question, "When?"

But let's now leave the question "When?" and go to "Who?" in verse 2. In answer, we have Nicodemus, Jesus, God, we, one. You could say, "Who is Jesus?" From that you start developing questions about Jesus and God. If you have a fairly good biblical background, you would not have so many questions, or at least the same type of questions as someone who had little biblical knowledge.

Let's ask the "Who?" question of the word "we" in verse 2. Who does the "we" refer to? This is the situation: A man by the name of Nicodemus, who was a pharisee, a ruler, a Jew and a teacher, came to Jesus at night and said, "We know."

The "we" could be (1) the Pharisees—Nicodemus could have been saying, "We Pharisees," "We religious leaders." Who else could it refer to? Perhaps it was (2) the teachers. Let's say you are a student at a university. Some famous person comes through, or someone who is causing a lot of commotion. Whom do you think the students would go to and ask questions about the celebrity? They would ask their professors. Don't you think the students were asking their teachers about this Jesus? So, maybe Nicodemus was referring to (3) himself and the students. Or maybe he was saying (4) "We Jews." Maybe he referred to (5) himself and his fellow rulers. Put yourself in his position. If I were a Pharisee, whom would I represent? If I were a leader of the Jews, whom would I represent? If I were a teacher, whom would I represent?

Who else could "we" refer to? Maybe he was just referring to (6) himself and trying to get off the hook. Often a person will exclaim, "Why, *everyone* knows!" or, *"We all know!"* when in reality he is the one asking the question and is simply using "we" or "everyone" as a smokescreen.

KNOW WHAT TO LOOK FOR

See what we have observed just by asking who the "we" refers to? As you start the steps of interpretation, you will begin to see the answer or at least narrow down the options.

You can see how it's possible to take these six observation questions and spend 10, 20, or 30 hours on just 10 verses! You would discover things you had overlooked in the past.

You probably are saying "But I don't have that much time!" If that is the case, allot the time you do have. Maybe you have only 10 minutes. But in that 10 minutes, if you ask these questions, you are going to find out more than if you did not ask the questions! This is a key point. Simply spend the time that you do have. Maybe you have 20 minutes, a half hour, or 45 minutes. Maybe you have a 50-minute plane ride. Ask: Who? What? When? Where? Why? How? for 50 minutes.

Let's say you are in a group Bible study or studying with another person and the study gets bogged down. You whip out your mental notebook—and ask some questions: Who? What? When? Where? Why? and How? You say, "All right, who is it talking about here?" "Okay, Janet, what is taking place?" "Describe it in your own words, Jim." "When did it take place, Pat?" They will think you are profound!

Assignment

1. Make observations from John 9 using the six questions, and put them into your observation chart.
2. From your observations, write down at lease 10 interpretive questions from John 9.

▼ *C H A P T E R   F O U R* ▼

More to Look For

- RELATIONSHIP QUESTIONS

From our initial six questions, let's go to the next 12 questions on structure, or relationships. They are:

1. Are there things that are alike?
2. Are there things that are different (contrasts, signaled by not, but, however)?
3. Are there things that are repeated (Hebrews 11: "By faith")?
4. Is there cause and effect?
5. Is there movement from general to specific (Acts 4-5; John 4)?
6. Is there a progression (may come in form of climax, such as persecution)?
7. Are there any questions or answers (2 Corinthians/whole book; Romans 6:1, 15)?
8. Is there a problem and a solution?
9. Is there emphasis by space (Genesis)?
10. Are there connectors (connectives and prepositions: but, since, therefore, if, and)?
11. Are there any commands?
12. Are there any promises?

You say, "Wow, that is a lot!" No, it isn't. You can go through our first six questions and these 12 relationships in

John 3:1-10 in 30 minutes. Or you can spend as much as 25 hours — if you have that much time — on these same questions. You don't believe me? I know of one person who made over 600 legitimate observations on one verse! Can you believe it? The verse was Acts 1:8.

The primary difference between the six initial questions and the above 12 structural questions is one of progression of knowledge. The relationship of two or more terms or people is now being examined.

The observations you make by asking these 12 questions also go in the center column of your observation chart.

Let's take a closer look at these relationship (structural) questions.

1. *Are there things that are alike or similar?* Look for comparisons. Now remember, the reason people do not see things is that they do not know what to look for. And all these questions are doing is giving you things to look for. That is the key. And so, if you are looking for things that are alike, you are more apt to see them.

Comparisons show that things are alike or similar. Study the reasons they are similar. Although we will see strong contrasts between John 3 and 4, what makes those contrasts stand out so strongly are the similarities between these two witnessing opportunities which Christ had. For example: (1) Both involved religious people. (2) Both were individual witnessing opportunities. (3) Both people were personally interested in spiritual things. (4) Christ guided the conversation to the key issue in both cases. (5) Christ took the initiative to point the issue to spiritual things in both cases. (6) Christ did not get sidetracked with side issues such as "miracles" in John 3 or the "Jewish-Samaritan" controversy in John 4.

2. *Are there things that are different?* Watch for *contrasts* and things that are dissimilar. Ask, "Why are they different?" Is there a reason? They are often introduced by the words "but" or "however," with a change of subject.

KNOW YOUR BIBLE

As we apply the structural question on contrasts, we will notice in John 3 and 4 that there are many important differences between Nicodemus and the Samaritan woman. These contrasts open a whole vista of understanding as to why John has chapter 4 follow chapter 3.

Differences

John 3	John 4
A man	A woman
A Jew	A Samaritan
Socially accepted	Social outcast
Comes by night	Talk comes in day
Still questioning	Comes to faith
Judaism	Samaritanism
Religious leader	Religious pagan
Ashamed	Bold
Etc.	Etc.

(In the book of Galatians, Paul used the idea of contrast to build his whole case for the superiority of grace over legalism, of the Spirit over the flesh. That is an excellent study of contrast.)

3. *Are there things that are repeated?* Jesus said over and over in John, "Verily, I say unto you." Often words, phrases and ideas are repeated to aid learning or to add emphasis. The order of the items may be significant — there may be a progression from something lesser to something greater.

4. *Is there cause and effect?* If you see the effect, what is the cause? If you see the cause, what is the effect? Cause and effect means that one thing leads to another. This is often introduced by the words "because," "for," or "therefore." For example, if you get hit in the head with a baseball bat, it leads to a headache. The effect: a headache; the cause: a hit to the head with a baseball bat.

MORE TO LOOK FOR

One of the most pivotal sequences of cause and effect relationships found in the gospels hinges on Peter's confession of Christ's identity (Matthew 16, Mark 8, Luke 9). Once Peter acknowledged Christ as Messiah, Jesus' ministry seemed to shift in various ways. In fact, that shift unlocks much of the gospels' structure. After Peter's confession, Christ began to set His face toward Jerusalem and His future death, and He spent more time teaching His disciples. This is a dramatic example of cause (Peter's confession) and effect (shift in Christ's ministry).

The opportunities for study using this question are endless. The Word of God begins to unfold by looking for *cause and effect*.

Another example of this taken from a whole book is found in Ephesians. In chapters 1-3 we have the cause: "Our position in Jesus Christ." What is the effect of this position? The effect is that our practice, or conduct, should be different from the conduct of those who do not have such a position in Christ. This effect is found in chapters 4-6. So you see our conduct in the Spirit (4-6) depends on our calling, or position, in Christ (1-3). That is cause and effect.

5. *Is there movement from general to specific?* Hebrews 11 is a good example of this type of movement. At the beginning of the chapter, the author gives some general, universal principles concerning faith, and then he moves to specific examples of men in "Faith's Hall of Fame."

6. *Is there a progression?* Look for something building, developing, or unfolding. This is crucial. There are a great many examples of this in the Scriptures. Often progression will climax with a specific act. For example, in the gospels, Jesus' public ministry moved slowly toward His triumphal entry into Jerusalem, which preceded His passion week leading to His crucifixion. Here again, the events that came before the crucifixion were also a progression.

7. *Are there any questions or answers?* Be alert for questions and answers in order to see how many arguments or conversations develop in the Scriptures (*see* John 3:4; Romans 6:1; 8:31-35; 11:34-35).

Questions force one to think, examine the issues, be specific, and stay on target. Thus you often see questions and answers being employed when one party or the other is attempting to drive a point home.

8. *Is there a problem and a solution?* Look for the use of problem and solution. Romans 1:1 is an example. "Paul, a bond-servant of Christ Jesus, called as an apostle, set apart for the gospel of God." Now, what was the problem behind this verse? The original readers might have questioned Paul's right to write Romans. Why, he had not even visited Rome or ministered there yet. "What authority do you have?" or "Why should you write Romans?" they might ask. So what did he do? He gave his credentials. The problem: They questioned his right to do it. The solution: He gave his credentials—he was a slave of Jesus Christ. He was also an apostle; that is a five-star general in the New Testament church. He was set apart by God for the gospel.

9. *Is there emphasis by space?* This is especially valuable when you study an entire book. For example, consider the book of Luke. In Luke 1:1-2:52, the time covered in Christ's life is about 30 years. In Luke 3:1-19:28, the time covered is about three years. But in Luke 19:29-24:53, the time covered is only *one week.* nearly 25 percent of Luke dwells on only one week of Christ's life, while only 8 percent deals with the time before His public ministry began.

Genesis is another good example of this principle. The book breaks down:

Creation of World	Abraham, Isaac, Jacob	Creation of Nation Joseph
Genesis 1—11	12—36	37—50

10. *Are there connectors?* Look for connectors and prepositions such as *"but," "since," "if," "therefore," "and,"* and so on. Those key words offer you clues about why the author said what he did. Words such as "since," "because," and "therefore" remind us of cause and effect.

Consider *conditional* connectives. You have "If — then" statements which set down specific conditions of fulfillment. *If* you do certain things, *then* God will do certain things. "If we confess our sins, [then] He is faithful and righteous to forgive us our sins and to cleanse us from all unrighteousness" (1 John 1:9). These "If — then" statements are found throughout the Word of God. So often, we give promises to people that are conditional promises. We need to look at God's conditions.

What about *connectives of purpose*? Look for phrases such as "in order that" or "because of." They open up the idea of purpose, or reason. Look at Philippians 3:12: "Not that I have already obtained it or have already become perfect, but I press on [Why does he press on? Reason or purpose:] in order that I may lay hold of that for which also I was laid hold of by Christ Jesus."

Look also for the *connectives indicating results*. The word "therefore" is excellent. It gives you results. The word "finally" also often indicates a result. Philippians 3:1, "Finally, my brethren, rejoice in the Lord." The result of all Paul said in bringing unity to the Philippians is to rejoice in the Lord.

The following is a list of various connectors for you to look for, along with their significance.

SIGNIFICANT WORDS TO LOOK FOR

1. Logical connectors:

    a. Contrast . . . . but (Ephesians 2:4)
                                  even though (Romans 1:21)
                                    much more (Romans 5:15)
                                    nevertheless (Ephesians 5:33)
                                    yet (Romans 5:8)
                                    although
                                    then
                                    otherwise (Romans 11:6)

    b. Comparison . . . . too (Ephesians 2:3)
                                    also (Ephesians 1:11)
                                    as (Ephesians 5:22)
                                    just as (Ephesians 4:32)
                                    so also (Ephesians 5:28)
                                    likewise (1 Peter 3:7)
                                    and
                                    like

    c. Correlatives . . . . as . . . so also (Ephesians 5:24)
                                    for . . . as (Ephesians 5:23)
                                    so . . . as (Ephesians 5:28)

    d. Reason . . . . because (Ephesians 2:4)
                                    for this reason . . . . (Ephesians 3:15)
                                    for this purpose (Ephesians 6:22)
                                    for (Ephesians 2:8)
                                    since (Colossians 1:4)

    e. Result . . . . so then (Ephesians 2:19)
                                    therefore (Ephesians 2:11)
                                    as a result (Ephesians 4:14)
                                    thus
                                    then

    f. Purpose/Result . . . . that (Ephesians 1:4)
                                    so that (Ephesians 1:18)
                                    in order that (Ephesians 4:28)

    g. Condition . . . . if (Ephesians 3:2)

2. Temporal or time connectors: now (Ephesians 2:2)
                                      until (Ephesians 4:13)
                                      when (Ephesians 1:20)
                                      before (Ephesians 1:4)
                                      after (Ephesians 1:13)
                                      while (Ephesians 1:16)
                                      since (Colossians 3:1)

3. Geographical connectors: where (Colossians 3:1)

11. *Are there any commands?* An obvious example is Matthew 28:19-20.

12. *Are there any promises?* Look for God's promises and consider also any conditions which may be attached to these promises (*see*, for example, 1 John 5:14-15).

Assignment

Make observations of John 9 using the 12 structural questions.

▼ CHAPTER FIVE ▼

See How It Works

Let's walk through part of John 4 and see just a few of the results of asking some of the 12 structural questions discussed in the last chapter. This will help you to see how they apply. I have probably spoken on John 4 more than on any other chapter in the Bible. I am looking forward to meeting that woman. I think that by the time I meet her, I can call her "lady."

Let's begin with one of the six basic questions: "What?" "What type of woman was she?" What do you do then? I have my observation chart, where there is space for the Scripture on the left, observations in the center, and interpretive questions on the right. I start to look for clues for determining *what* type of woman she was.

Asking this question led me to notice some of the characteristics of the woman. She was:

1. a prostitute or adulteress (v. 18). (Jesus said to her, "Go, call your husband" (v. 16). She said, "I have no husband" (v. 17). He said, "You have had five husbands; and the one whom you now have is not your husband" (v. 18). She was living in adultery.);
2. a religious formalist (v. 20);
3. a nationalist—proud of her heritage (v. 12);
4. sensitive to the race problem (v. 9);
5. did not like to draw water (v. 15);
6. hungry to know the Messiah (vv. 25, 28-29);
7. a Samaritan (v. 9).

SEE HOW IT WORKS

After looking at this list and reading the passage, ask yourself, "What were some of the differences between Jesus and the woman?"

1. She was a sinner, living in adultery. He was the holy Son of God, a righteous man. You could write down "Rabbi."
2. She was a woman; He was a man.
3. He was a Jew, and what was she? A Samaritan! They were from different races.
4. She was of the Samaritan religion. He was of the Jewish religion.
5. He was from Judah; she was from Samaria.

These are a few of the differences between them.

The areas of differences immediately trigger the question, "What barriers were there between Jesus and this woman as a result of their differences?"

First, you have a *moral barrier*. Jesus was the holy, righteous Son of God. She was living in adultery.

Second, you have a *social barrier*. He was a man; she was a woman. The sexes did not mix in public, let alone privately. This is why in verse 27, when the disciples came back from the city, they marveled that He had been speaking with a woman.

Third, she was a Samaritan; He was a Jew. That was a *racial barrier*.

Fourth, she was of the Samaritan religion; He was of the Jewish religion. That was a *religious barrier*.

Fifth, the fact that she was from Samaria and He was from Judah constituted a *political barrier*.

Incredible! All this comes from asking questions (and having experience in studying the Bible). *You* can have that same "experience," but it takes time and effort.

KNOW YOUR BIBLE

Differences

Woman	Jesus	Barrier
1. Adulteress (v.18)	1. Rabbi (v.31)_____	1. Moral
2. Woman (v.9)	2. Man (v.9)_____	2. Social
3. Samaritan (v.9)	3. Jewish (v.9)_____	3. Racial
4. Samaritan religion	4. Judaism_____	4. Religious
5. From Samaria	5. From Judah_____	5. Political

Notice how Jesus broke down these barriers:

1. *He went out of His way and broke many long-standing traditions.* "And He had to pass through Samaria" (v.4). He went out of His way to meet and talk to this Samaritan woman. Samaria was a section of Palestine, and if a Jew had business on the other side of Samaria, instead of passing through it, he would walk all the way around it to keep from touching Samaritan soil. There was hatred between the Samaritans and the Jews. This deep prejudice issued from several causes:

   a. The Assyrians captured Samaria in 722 B.C. and took many people into exile. However, at the same time, many Assyrians came to live in Samaria. It did not take long for the Jews in Samaria to begin marrying the Assyrians. That was unthinkable to the other Jews. The result was a mixed race despised by the Jews of Jerusalem.

   b. In A.D. 6 and 9, the Samaritans went to Jerusalem and scattered bones in the sacred area of the temple. That was an abomination to the Jews.

   c. The Samaritans used the first five books of the Old Testament for their Bible. However, they changed the place of worship from Jerusalem to Mt. Gerizim. This tampering with the sacred Scriptures caused an obsessive hatred of the Samaritans.

2. Jesus asked the woman for a favor. He asked help from her. "There came a woman of Samaria to draw water. Jesus said to her, 'Give Me a drink'" (v.7). There are several ways to get people to like you when you first meet them, and one is to ask them to help you. That way they feel you are indebted to them and not vice versa. Basically, people like to help others. It makes them feel good.

The next question you might ask is about progression. Is there an indication of progression in John 4? Notice the progression of Jesus' witness to her, the method of presenting the gospel. Jesus used four progressive principles in order to break down the multitude of barriers and win this adulteress, a Samaritan, to God:

1. He offered her something desirable (vv.10, 13-14). What was one of the most desirable things this woman wanted? It was water in her house, so she would not have to come out in the hot sun to draw water and face the ridicule of the other women. Jesus said the water He could give would cause her never to thirst again. Now, to that woman, this was desirable; for the woman answered, "Sir, give me this water, so I will not be thirsty, nor come all the way here to draw" (v.15). She did not understand then the spiritual significance of what Jesus said.

2. He told her why she could not have the thing desired. He exposed her sin. Jesus replied to the woman's inquiry about the water by saying, "Go, call your husband, and come here" (v.16). She responded immediately, "I have no husband" (v.17). Jesus corrected her saying, "You have well said, 'I have no husband'; for you have had five husbands; and the one whom you now have is not your husband; this you have said truly" (vv.17-18).

The woman started to get the point. Jesus was some sort of religious man— perhaps a fanatic. She said, "Sir, I perceive that You are a prophet. Our fathers worshipped in this mountain; and you people say that in Jerusalem is the place where men ought to worship" (vv.19-20). Her reaction was sullen withdrawal. Immediately she was evasive and became argumentative when He touched the moral realm.

Like many others when the moral position is challenged, she took refuge in arguing impersonally about religion. She immediately sought to divert His inquiry into the moral area by asking Him the question that for years had divided Jews from Samaritans—what was the place of worship?

What did Jesus do? He did not argue with her. I am sure He could have put up quite an argument. In fact, I would have liked to have heard it. But He did not argue. Instead, He replied to the deeper personal need concealed behind her intellectual question.

I have found in my experience that people today do the same thing. They try to avoid the moral issue. They often come up with intellectual questions or problems that have been argued for ages.

For this reason, very seldom do I answer questions put to me by those I am witnessing to. Why? Most of the time they are not relevant, and they are peripheral questions. They usually ask a question or state something that they heard someone else ask. Usually I only have a short time to talk with the person and do not want to be side-tracked.

Therefore, I compliment the person: "That is a good question," (if it really is) "but why don't we wait until I finish, and I will answer it for you." Unless it is a very crucial or bothersome question, they say, "That's fine." Usually they forget the question by the time you finish.

If the question bothers them, I answer it immediately. If not, I postpone it. We can spend a lot of time on intellectual arguments and never lead a soul to Christ. But we need to be willing always to answer a pressing question someone might have.

One time I was talking to a student and said, "God loves you and has a wonderful plan for your life."

He said, "I've got a question! How do you know there is a God?"

I replied, "That is a good question; why don't you wait until we finish the *Four Spiritual Laws*, and I will answer it for you."

He said, "OK."

When I got to the third law, I spent more time than usual explaining why Jesus was the Son of God. Later that student prayed to receive Jesus as Savior and Lord. I could have gone through the various arguments for the existence of God (anthropological, cosmological, teleological, etc.), and never led him to Christ. Do not argue. Talk about Jesus.

3. Next, Jesus related to the Samaritan woman God's plan of salvation and worship (vv.22-24). Now, He must have said more than this, and it was left out of the written conversation for she replied, "I know that Messiah is coming (He who is called Christ); when that One comes, He will declare all things to us" (v.25). From that part of the conversation, we see that she knew salvation was through Christ, the Messiah.

4. Finally, He directly challenged her personal faith. Would she believe or not? "Jesus said to her, 'I who speak to you am He'" (v.26).

Summary of progression: Jesus first offered her something desirable; then He told her why she could not have it. He then related God's plan of salvation through Christ, and finally made it personal and challenged her to make a decision.

KNOW YOUR BIBLE

It is because of these four points that I like the *Four Spiritual Laws* used by Campus Crusade for Christ. They are biblical. They start out with something desirable (Law 1). *God loves you, and offers a wonderful plan for your life.*

The word for *gospel* in Greek in "euaggelion," and it means "good news." Most plans of evangelism begin by saying that man is a sinner. Let me ask you, how many of you thought it was good news when you found out you were a sinner?

There are two things people are looking for today that would be good news to them (as living water was to the woman at the well). The first is love and the second is a plan for their lives, a purpose to live for.

In Law 2, we are told the reason we cannot experience the first law. *Man is sinful and separated from God. Therefore, he cannot know and experience God's love and plan for his life.*

Then in Law 3 we have God's plan for salvation. *Jesus Christ is God's only provision for man's sin. Through Him you can know and experience God's love and plan for your life.*

Then we have the need to make it personal and call for a decision (Law 4). *We must individually receive Jesus Christ as Savior and Lord; then we can know and experience God's love and plan for our lives.*

(To obtain a copy of the *Four Spiritual Laws* booklet, contact your Christian bookstore or Here's Life Publishers.)

You also see a progression in the woman's attitude toward Christ after He talked with her: In verse 9 she called Him a Jew, a slanderous term to a Samaritan; in verse 11 she said, "Sir"—a polite term. In verse 19 she referred to him as a prophet, and then in verse 29 she proclaimed that He was the Christ. There was a progression of respect and admiration in her reaction to Christ.

Then there was also a *progression* in the evangelistic results: (1) She met Christ (v.26), (2) She told others in a matter of

minutes (v.29). (3) Others believed: "And from that city many
of the Samaritans believed in Him because of the word of the
woman who testified" (v.39). (4) And finally, "And many more
believed because of His word" (v.41).

These observations produce many interpretive questions:
How did Jesus break those barriers down? Were the barriers
significant? Who was a Samaritan? How did a person become a
Samaritan? Where is Samaria? What was the Samaritans' relationship to the Jews? What was the Samaritan religion? What
did they worship? What were their religious books? Do you see
all the questions you can ask right here? You record these questions in the right-hand, "Interpretive Questions" column of
your Observation Chart. Then you take the steps of interpretation to find the answers.

Notice the *cause and effect* in verse 26. The effect was, as we
have seen, that she dropped her pot and ran into the city. What
was the cause? Jesus had confronted her with Himself. She told
the people about Christ. What was the effect? Not only did the
woman come to Christ, but also many of the men of the city
came out to see Him.

In John 4:28, only a woman was with Jesus, but by John 4:30
a whole town was with him! What happened? That sole
woman's testimony was the cause that brought the whole town
out to Jesus. What an incredible impact! And all this insight is
gained by asking the question, "Is there cause and effect?"

Now, let's see the movement from *general to specific*. Jesus
opened the conversation by asking for a drink. But then He told
her He could give her water that would cause her never to thirst
again. He started with water in general — with a secular
connotation — and then He went to water with a spiritual
significance. From there, He went to the Father (v.23). And
then, from the Father, He went to the Son (v.25-26).

I remember one time we were driving past all those steel
mills in Gary, Indiana, and I had a non-Christian fellow with
me. I said, "Wow! Look at all those steel mills!"

"Yeah, I'd like to own them!" he said.

"My Father does," I replied.

"He does?" was the startled response.

"Yeah, My Father in heaven. You see, He owns everything!" I started out general—secular—and moved to the spiritual in the specific. That is a key principle in evangelism.

I walked into a discount store once in La Mirada, California, and there was a watch repairman. I handed him my watch and said, "Sir, would you please buff the crystal?"

He said yes and turned on a buffer.

Then I said, "Hey, be careful. My Father owns this store."

He immediately turned the buffer off and said, "He does?"

I replied, "Yeah, my Father in heaven. You see, I became a child of God on December 19, 1959, at 8:30 at night."

And it ended up that he prayed to trust Christ and has since become a dear friend and supporter. I started out with the general, then moved to the specific. You know where I got that idea? John 4.

What about *question and answer?* Go to John 4:35: "Do you not say, 'There are yet four months, and then comes the harvest'?" That is obviously a question. So I asked myself, Who asked that question? Who does the question go back to? The disciples. Jesus indicated that they were more concerned about food for their bellies than they were about the work of winning souls. In other words, the question actually came from what Jesus knew was in the minds of the disciples.

You can analyze the question this way. The disciples were preoccupied with material things and did not see the spiritual need around them that Jesus was working to meet. They thought His main work as Messiah, the overthrow of Roman rule, was still to come. But what did Jesus see? He saw immense spiritual need, a longing for forgiveness of sins, and a great many people ready to receive the gospel. So He tried to point the disciples attention to this immediate spiritual harvest ready to be picked. I got all this by asking a question and seeking an answer.

I think there is a difference between friendship evangelism and aggressive evangelism. I love friendship evangelism. If people are not ready to hear the gospel, I build a relationship with them. If they are ready to trust Christ, I pray with them and build a relationship with them. Either way, if time permits, you build a relationship with them.

The disciples were only concerned at that moment with eating. But Jesus said their priorities and focus were wrong. Rather than being concerned about food, Jesus told them, "I have food to eat that you do not know about" (4:32). The disciples were saying to one another, "No one brought him anything to eat, did he?" And Jesus said to them, "My food is to do the will of Him who sent me and to accomplish His work" (v. 34). His work was basically preaching the gospel and dying for our sins. That's what He came for, to share Himself.

Now, who was He addressing? The disciples. Jesus understood their question, even though it was not explicitly stated. They were questioning His not eating and in so doing they were overlooking the spiritual harvest ready all around them. He said, "Lift up your eyes, and look on the fields, that they are white for harvest" (v. 35).

Those words left an impression on the disciples. They saw the harvest, and the harvest was people. They were the people the woman went to and said, "Come, see a man who told me all the things that I have done; this is not the Christ, is it?" And they came to listen to Him for themselves.

It does not take long before you have pages of observations and questions from what you have seen. Where do we go from here? The next step is interpretation.

One important point, though, before we move on. Do *not* try to draw a rigid distinction between observation and interpretation. For in one sense, much of your observation has interpretation built into it. What do I mean?

For example, you observed that Nicodemus was a Pharisee. Write that down as an observation. Now you could ask, "What is a Pharisee?" That is an interpretive question. And if you looked up the answer in a Bible dictionary, you would have an interpretation, an answer, or the meaning. *However*, if you just continued to make observations, you could discover that a Pharisee was a ruler of the Jews, a leader, a member of the synagogue, and so on, all from just observation. So you see that there is a partial blending of observation and interpretation. The interpretation step helps us to answer more fully the question of meaning.

Assignment

On John 9 write down 10 interpretive questions from the observations previously made.

▼ STEP FOUR ▼

Interpretation
"Know It"

▼ CHAPTER SIX ▼

Start Looking for Answers

Recently a young man said to me, "There are so many inter-pretations of the Bible — what am I supposed to believe? I can believe anything I want." Have you heard that before? It is one of the tricks Satan uses to confuse people and keep them from studying the Bible.

Interpretation may be defined as: "The process of determin-ing the meaning of the text." What is the real goal of interpreta-tion? It is to understand what the passage means.

What we want to do, then, is discover and understand what the human author, who was divinely inspired, meant by certain statements. The human author wrote under the influence of the Spirit of God, so when you discover what the human author meant, you discover what the divine author meant.

And when Jesus says "I am the bread of life," does it mean He is a loaf of bread? Of course not! It is a metaphor saying that Jesus provides sustenance for our spiritual life as a loaf of bread provides sustenance for our physical life. The answer here seems so obvious because *we do* (you do!) have a basic knowledge of how to interpret Scripture.

START LOOKING FOR ANSWERS

- ### UNLOCKING INTERPRETATION

Among other things, the Bible is literature, and the same principles that apply to the understanding of any other literature apply also to the Word of God. The basic difference between other literature and the Bible is validity. All Scripture is true, but not all literature is true. Thus, the Bible is easier to interpret because you do not have the additional step of trying to determine what is true and what is not. Yet, this major difference of truth makes the interpretation rich, since the Word is without error, it was inspired by God, it is powerful and it has authority that no other literature has.

The Bible was written in history and it uses grammar, and we must understand both of those to get the right meaning. Is that difficult? No! Let's consider the previous example of "the bread of life" (John 6:35).

"I am the bread of life" was stated in the historical background of Israel, during Roman times. At that time, bread was a main source of food. The grammar shows us that Jesus said it in the present tense: He "is," not "was," the bread of life. Greek literary tradition is very rich, and the use of metaphors such as this one was common.

But how do we find the answers to our questions, the proper interpretation of these things? What are the steps we take? Well, we have already formulated the interpretive questions in the observation chart, questions such as "What does it mean?" and "Why is it there?" The next steps will help us unlock the history, the grammar, and the literature behind a scriptural passage. Remember that our goal in interpretation of Scripture is to *know it!*

The Bible was written not only in a historical, but also a cultural setting. As literature, it has figures of speech, prose, poetry, drama, narrative, and so on. Its grammar includes questions, commands, verb tenses, and all the things grammar involves.

KNOW YOUR BIBLE

If we did not interpret the Bible using these three areas (history, grammar and literature), we could make the Bible say anything we wanted it to! But that is not our goal. Rather, we want to learn what God said and what He meant. This understanding comes from Scripture the same way it comes from anything else that is written. Normally we understand what we read without ever considering how, but we use the process involving the three areas named above.

Before we move into the steps toward achieving our goal in interpretation, let's examine its importance.

• THE IMPORTANCE OF ACCURATE INTERPRETATION

The Jehovah's Witnesses teach that Jesus Christ is not the incarnate Son of God, God come in human flesh. We Christians teach that He is. Who is right? Someone is. Both teachings cannot be true. This is an important fact. Either Christ is the Son of God or He is not. If He is not, there is a variety of possible interpretations of who He was, including that of the Witnesses. But this claim of divine Sonship is exclusive. The answer is a matter of interpretation, and it happens to be a major theme of the Gospel of John — the divine identity of the Son.

Improper interpretation leads to misconception and false teaching. You cannot believe the Bible any way you want. There is not a myriad of valid interpretations. That is our culture talking.

People say, "That's great if it's true for you, but it's not true for me." Or they say, "The Bible speaks to me differently here. The important thing is how *I* understand it." No! The Bible speaks truth as it is written; its truth does not depend on how we see it. For example, Jesus Christ lived, taught, was crucified, and rose again independent of whether I believe it or not or if I think it is true for me. Christ is either God the Son or He is not. The Bible is God's Word or it is not.

Our culture also teaches how difficult it is to understand a book like the Bible, which is so old and is a religious book besides. But the fact is that the Bible is not hard for a person to understand. You do not need seminary, Bible school, Hebrew or Greek. I am not saying those disciplines are not of great value and extreme benefit in studying and teaching the Scriptures. They are important. What I am saying is that they are not absolutely necessary to gleaning the truth and meaning of God's Word. Also, those who have put forth the effort to study it confirm that it is very understandable.

Second Timothy 3:16-17 says, "All Scripture is inspired by God and profitable for teaching, for reproof, for correction, for training in righteousness; that the man of God may be adequate, equipped for every good work." And this injunction is for all believers. The Word is full of its own teaching concerning its power and our need for it to be part of our lives. If the Word was so difficult to understand, why all the biblical commands to study the Scripture, commands that presuppose that we *can* understand it?

We all have the same Bible and the same Holy Spirit, and the Lord is interested in imparting truth to us all. The Word teaches that it is an open book to Christians — not only open, but even exciting, and the command is to know it and apply it. The problems come from those who try to make truth subject to their personal experiences or who try to bend truth to satisfy their personal goals rather than the Lord's.

Just for review, interpretation builds on the foundation of observation. Thorough observation makes interpretation easier. If you really see what the Bible says and bring together all the things you observe, you can interpret more accurately. Interpretation gets hard when you have looked at the Bible only casually.

The greater the quality of observation, the greater the accuracy of interpretation. That is why we spend so much time on looking and observing. As you continue to read this book, you will notice lots of ideas repeated. You may get tired of seeing the same things over and over, but repetition aids learning, and as we learn about observation, it will flow into interpretation. Many of the principles of observation are true also of interpretation—we are looking for details and want God to teach us.

Now let's look in the next two chapters at the process of interpretation. The process is simple but important. As we move through each step, you will find that your knowledge increases steadily. You will understand more, not only of what the author said, but of why he said it.

▼ *C H A P T E R   S E V E N* ▼

Start By Looking Elsewhere

Perhaps you have heard a preacher or teacher say that the Bible explains itself, or that you should not build a doctrine on just one passage of Scripture. The reason those statements are true is that the Bible usually does discuss a given important topic in more than one place. Thus, to understand one passage better, you can look for other passages that help explain it. These other passages are called cross-references.

To cross-reference, you go from one verse to another verse that is very similar, or contains the same word, and that usually will cast light upon whatever you are studying. So it is Scripture interpreting Scripture. And this is one of the most important steps in interpretation. To me, it is also one of the most enjoyable parts of Bible study.

The method in using cross-references is again to start with the big picture and then narrow it down. By pursuing the cross-references, we are able to shed light on the desired meaning of a word by gaining information from other parts of the Bible. Then when we come to the next steps, the *context* and *definitions*, we begin to narrow our scope, concentrating even more on the specific passage in question. Cross-references give us a solid foundation for the knowledge we seek.

You begin a cross-reference study by looking at the questions you raised in your observations. Guess what? You need another chart — two columns this time. The column on the left is where you record the verses you use in cross-referencing a

CROSS-REFERENCE CHART
(Word or Verse)

Cross-reference	Significance

START BY LOOKING ELSEWHERE

word or passage. In the column on the right, you have the point of significance. So across the top of the page you have the word or verses you are going to cross-reference, and the two columns you will have are titled "Cross-reference" and "Significance."

The cross-references I prefer are usually found in marginal references from the *New American Standard Bible.* Other versions also have various types of cross-references.

Take your NASB now and turn to John 3, and let's work through an example together. The marginal notes and cross-references in the NASB are usually placed in a column on the outer edge of the page or in a center column and listed under verse numbers to which they refer. Raised *letters* refer to cross-references. Cross-references in *italics* are parallel passages. Raised *numbers* refer to literal renderings, alternate translations or explanations.(See samples below)

29 ªJohn 19:29, 30; Matt. 27:48, 50; Mark 15:36f.; Luke 23:36

29 A jar full of sour wine was standing there; so ªthey put a sponge full of the sour wine upon *a branch of* hyssop, and brought it up to His mouth.

30 ªJohn 17:4 ᵇMatt. 27:50; Mark 15:37; Luke 23:46

30 When Jesus therefore had received the sour wine, He said, "ªIt is finished!" And He bowed His head, and ᵇgave up His spirit.

31 ¹Lit., *for the day of that Sabbath was great* ªJohn 19:14, 42 ᵇDeut. 21:23; Josh. 8:29; 10:26f. ᶜEx. 12:16

¶31 The Jews therefore, because it was ªthe day of preparation, so that ᵇthe bodies should not remain on the cross on the Sabbath (¹for that Sabbath was a ᶜhigh *day*), asked Pilate that their legs might be broken, and *that* they might be taken away.

However, the first word in John 3 that you will probably want to look up is "Pharisee," and there is no cross-reference listed for that. But, along with looking at the verses for words that are cross-referenced, you can also use a concordance for those that are not. A concordance is a book containing an alphabetical listing of all the words in the Bible, and it shows the context in which each word appears.

In this case, if you want more information on Pharisee, you will have to go to a concordance. You look up the title "Pharisee," and if yours is an exhaustive concordance, it will list all the verses where that word is used. It will give you a phrase to go with it, so you can get some understanding of what the verse is about. What I recommend when using a concordance is that you first look at all the references in the same book of the Bible. Then, after the same book, look at references in other

books by the same author. Then go from the same author to the
whole New Testament, if that is where the author is, and then
to the whole Bible. When you do not have a lot of time, it is better to have a particular author interpreting his own words. To
understand a word from the Gospel of John, for example, you
would go to 1 John, 2 John and 3 John.

Now, back to our example in John 3. One question that
arose in the interpretive questions column was, "Who are the
rulers?" We want to study the "rulers of the Jews" and see the
significance of Nicodemus' being a ruler. For John 3:1, we'll
write down "Ruler." You put it at the top of the cross-reference
chart in capital letters. Look at the word "ruler" in verse 1.
There's a small raised "b" to the left of the word in the text.
That refers you to the marginal reference. So, you go to the
marginal reference and you look for "1," which indicates cross-
references of verse 1. Then you find the raised "b." I want you to
do this with me. See where we have the raised "b" in the
margin? What reference does it say there? Luke 23:13, and John
7:26 and 48.

25 ªMatt. 9:4; John 1:42, 47;
6:61, 64; 13:11

1 ªJohn 7:50; 19:39 ᵇLuke
23:13; John 7:26, 48

2 ¹Or, *attesting miracles*
ªMatt. 23:7; John 3:26 ᵇJohn
2:11 ᶜJohn 9:33; 10:38;
14:10f.; Acts 2:22; 10:38

3 ¹Or, *from above*
ª2 Cor. 5:17; 1 Pet. 1:23
ᵇMatt. 19:24; 21:31; Mark
9:47; 10:14f.; John 3:5

CHAPTER 3

NOW there was a man of the Pharisees, named ªNico-
demus, a ᵇruler of the Jews;

2 this man came to Him by night, and said to Him,
"ªRabbi, we know that You have come from God *as* a teacher;
for no one can do these ¹ᵇsigns that You do unless ᶜGod is
with him."

3 Jesus answered and said to him, "Truly, truly, I say to
you, unless one ªis born ¹again, he cannot see ᵇthe kingdom of
God."

4 Nicodemus ªsaid to Him, "How can a man be born
when he is old? He cannot enter a second time into his mother's womb and be born, can he?"

Go to the cross-reference chart, to the left-hand column titled "cross-reference," and write down Luke 23:13. Then turn
to Luke 23:13: "And Pilate summoned the chief priests and the
rulers and the people." What does this verse bring out about the
rulers? Any significance here? Yes, there was some sort of relationship with Pilate, or Pilate had authority over them.

What else do you find in Luke 23:13? There are both chief

START BY LOOKING ELSEWHERE

priests and rulers, and they are different. You can write down, "categories: chief priests and rulers." Already, we have seen Pharisees and rulers (John 3:1). Now, we add another category, "chief priests." We recognize that there are at least three types of positions in the hierarchy of Israel.

Now notice next to the word "rulers" in verse 13 that there is a small elevated "a" that indicates further references for "ruler." You are next going to look up all the cross-references from Luke 23:13 *before* you go back to the original John 3:1 reference.

13 ᵃActs 4:27

13 ᵃLuke 23:35; John 7:26, 48; 12:42; Acts 3:17; 4:5, 8; 13:27

¶13 And Pilate summoned the chief priests and the ᵃrulers and the people,

14   and said to them, "You brought this man to me as one who ᵃincites the people to rebellion, and behold, having examined Him before you, I ᵇhave found no guilt in this man regarding the charges which you make against Him.

You go to the margin under 13, little "a," and it says Luke 23:35. Write down Luke 23:35 in the cross-reference chart. Then read 23:35: "And the people stood by, looking on. And even the rulers were sneering at Him, saying, 'He saved others; let Him save Himself if this is the Christ of God, His Chosen One.'" What do we learn about the rulers from this verse? They were sneering at Christ. Maybe that is why Nicodemus came at night, because of the rulers' sneering at Jesus.

In Luke 23:35, is there another cross-reference for "ruler"? It says Luke 23:13. We have seen that already, so there is no further cross-reference for this study in verse 35.

¶33 ᵃAnd when they came to the place called ¹The Skull, there they crucified Him and the criminals, one on the right and the other on the left.

34 ¹But Jesus was saying, "ᵃFather, forgive them; for they do not know what they are doing." ᵇAnd they cast lots, dividing up His garments among themselves.

35 And the people stood by, looking on. And even the ᵃrulers were sneering at Him, saying, "He saved others; ᵇlet Him save Himself if this is the ¹Christ of God, His Chosen One."

35 ¹I.e., Messiah
ᵃLuke 23:13 ᵇMatt. 27:43

36 ᵃMatt. 27:48

37 ᵃMatt. 27:43

38 ᵃMatt. 27:37; Mark 15:26; John 19:19

What verse do we go back to now? Luke 23:13! You should look up all references in Luke 23:13 before you go back to John 3:1, where we started. When you go back to Luke 23:13, it says to see John 7:26. So, you write down John 7:26.

Now, you turn to John 7:26: "And look, He is speaking publicly, and they are saying nothing to Him. The rulers do not really know that this is the Christ, do they?" Here you could bring out that the rulers were ignorant about Jesus. Perhaps Nicodemus, representing the rulers, was going to Jesus to get some things cleared up. But here, they had some questions and did not seem to know that He was the Christ. In other words, it appears that the rulers as a whole did not believe in Him as the Christ.

The next cross-reference available is John 7:48. It says, "No one of the rulers or Pharisees has believed in Him, has he?" What is the point of significance here? You see, if there were any believers among the rulers, they were silent believers. Look at the context. In looking at a cross-reference, always take into consideration the verses before and after.

"The officers therefore came to the chief priests and Pharisees, and they said to them, 'Why did you not bring Him?' The officers answered, 'Never did a man speak the way this man speaks.' The Pharisees therefore answered them, 'You have not also been led astray, have you? No one of the rulers or Pharisees has believed in Him, has he? But this multitude which does not know the Law is accursed.' Nicodemus said to them (he who came to Him before, being one of them), 'Our Law does not judge a man, unless it first hears from him and knows what he is doing, does it?' They answered and said to him, 'You are not also from Galilee, are you? Search, and see that no prophet arises out of Galilee'" (John 7:45-52).

Verses before: The officers came back and the chief priests and Pharisees said, "Where is this fellow? We sent you out to get Jesus, and you come back and say, 'Never did a man speak the way this man speaks.'" The Pharisees therefore answered them, "You have not also been led astray, have you?"

START BY LOOKING ELSEWHERE

In the verses after, those same rulers said that the multitudes who believed in Jesus did not know the Law and were accursed. Nicodemus then said they ought not to judge a man unless they first heard from him and knew what he was doing.

What did they then accuse Nicodemus of? Becoming one of His followers. Did Nicodemus point out that he had gone to talk to Jesus? No. He kept it silent. There was a fear there of the rulers. Why did he not say, "Look, I went and talked to Him and this is what He said..."? He played the whole role as if he had never been there. And yet, the Scriptures point out that it was "he who came to Him by night." Thus, Nicodemus was afraid to speak up in the presence of the rulers and the Pharisees about his visit with Jesus.

As you study further, you see the word "rulers" with a reference to John 12:42. That verse says: "Nevertheless many even of the rulers believed in Him, but because of the Pharisees they were not confessing Him, lest they should be put out of the synagogue." This may shed more light on why Nicodemus visited Jesus by night. It shows that the Pharisees had authority over the rulers when it came to religious things. They could throw them out of the synagogue. And it shows that a number of the rulers did believe but were not confessing Him.

Usually, I do not go more than three generations of references from the original (in our case, John 3:1). After three generations, time usually becomes a factor. If you have the time, and you are going to be teaching the subject, you may want to go further. (Notice that under Luke 23:13 these further references are given: Acts 3:17; 4:5,8; 13:27.) You could spend your entire lifetime just doing cross-reference studies! You can find out what the Bible itself says about the different subjects and the different phrases you are studying.

When you exhaust all further references in Luke 23:13, where do you go? Back to John 3:1. At John 3:1, it says see John 7:26. We have seen that. Then it says see John 7:48. We have seen that. At this point, we have exhausted the cross-references.

▼ STEP FOUR ▼
KNOW YOUR BIBLE

You might be saying, "This takes a lot of time." But look, if you only have 15 minutes, just take 15 minutes. If you have two hours, take two hours. This is something you can do while traveling in a bus or sitting in a doctor's office — no matter where you are, you can do it. All you need is a Bible with cross-references, paper, and pen.

CROSS-REFERENCE CHART

John 3:1
Student Sample

Cross-reference	Significance

"Ruler"
Luke 23:13
	Relationship with Pilate
	Categories
	    Chief priest
	    Rulers

Luke 23:35	Sneered at Jesus
John 7:26	Rulers didn't believe in Christ
John 7:48	Nicodemus afraid to speak of his relationship to Jesus
John 12:42	Many rulers believe in Jesus — never said so out of fear of Pharisees. Pharisees could put them out of the synagogue.
Acts 3:17	Peter points out "rulers" acted in ignorance concerning Christ just as he did.
Acts 4:5,8	Two more categories: elders and scribes. After 500 believed, the rulers and others gathered with the high priest asked Peter questions.
Acts 13:27	Paul exhorted Jewish leaders in the synagogue. He says neither the people nor their rulers recognized Him or His teachings.

Assignment

Do a cross-reference of a word in John 9. It is best not to go over one page at this point unless you have time.

▼ *CHAPTER EIGHT* ▼

Looking Closer to Home

- CONTEXT

From cross-references we move to the context, the verses both preceding and following the passage under study.

Notice we have a lot of charts. Why? A chart keeps you organized. And what we develop now is the interpretation chart, or outline. You need more 8 1/2 X 11 sheets of paper. You will use this outline for the rest of the steps in interpretation.

At the top of the page, just put "INTERPRETATIONS." Under that main heading write the sub-title, "Context." Now you are ready to check out the context of your passage. If you are doing rulers of the Jews, you go to the chapter in which that appears. Turn again to John 3:1-10 and look at the verses before and after. Do they add anything? If they do have any significance, write it down under "Context."

Context is so important. Many errors people make in studying the Bible are due to the fact that they ignore the context. One classic example I have seen many times in a university classroom is when students study the Bible as literature and pit James against Paul on the issue of faith and works. James says in chapter 2, verse 17 of his epistle that faith without works is dead. Yet Paul in Ephesians 2 and Galatians 3 makes it clear that faith, not works, is the means to salvation. Is there a scriptural contradiction? No. The verses are taken out of context. First, James' point is that faith has action associated with it.

Talk is cheap, he says. Second, Paul's subject is salvation, while James' is sanctification, or your Christian walk. They are entirely different issues, and the passages must be understood contextually in order to grasp what the Bible teaches on faith.

• DEFINITIONS

Then, from the context, go to the dictionary. Write down the word *definitions*. I usually box it in. Why? So it will jump off the page. I will know what that section is talking about.

Start with a *secular dictionary*. It is amazing what you can learn about biblical words in a secular dictionary. In fact, often it will give you the biblical meaning. The dictionary ties you in with the background of the word, where it comes from. Then, write down the meaning on the interpretation sheet and document it. Be careful of your documentation. You need to know where your material comes from in case someone asks you a question. Sometimes you will not be able to document, but try your best.

Next, go to a Bible dictionary and write out that definition. You need a good one. *Unger's Bible Dictionary* is one I like. It brings in a lot of archaeology. Then, if it is true that a picture is worth a thousand words, there is *Zondervan's Pictorial Encyclopedia of the Bible*. Some of the most thorough are the *New Bible Dictionary* and the new Tyndale three-volume *Illustrated Bible Dictionary*.

Any of these will give you the background of the word, the Old Testament usage, the New Testament usage, the historical meaning and other important facts. Write down anything the Bible dictionary brings out that is significant to the passage you are studying. Do not forget to document it so you know where it came from.

When using a dictionary, do not look up only the word you are studying, but also look up synonyms, antonyms, and corresponding words. For example, if you are studying love, look up hate. If you are studying Pharisee, look up Sadducee. It will throw light on the word you are studying. If you are studying teacher, look up education, also Jewish education. It will give you a broader idea as to who a Jewish teacher was, an understanding you would not get by just looking up teacher.

- ## TRANSLATIONS — PARAPHRASES

The next step is to check different Bible translations and paraphrases. This will greatly expand your understanding of the text, especially in the area of application and the formulating of biblical principles. Look at two or three translations and paraphrases. My two favorite paraphrases are, *The Amplified Bible* and *The Living Bible*. I also often use J.B. Phillips' paraphrase or *Good News for Modern Man*. Do not base doctrine on a paraphrase, however. Base doctrine on a translation. I appreciate the *New American Standard Bible*, and the *New International Version* is a worthwhile translation.

You may pick up a little different meaning from reading paraphrases. They often will give you a new insight into a passage or the use of a specific word. Write out what you observe.

- ## REFERENCE BOOKS

The next step in the process of interpretation is examining the various excellent and helpful reference books. These give the scholarly insights of experts. They are not always correct in what they say. This is why you should consider them last and weigh what they say in light of the biblical observations you have already made. Yet you can learn a lot as you go to them for contributions. Often they supply information to help you understand the passage rather than simply giving you the interpretation.

Many people, believing it to be more spiritual, dogmatically say they do not go to any book but the Bible itself. They will often proclaim they are "so led of the Spirit" that they do not need other books to understand the Bible. To me, this borders on spiritual arrogance. The Bible is very clear that God has given us "teachers" along with the other gifts to build up the "body." What better way to pass on this marvelous spiritual gift of teaching than by the printed page? I have always wondered why those who are so against other books encourage people to listen to their expounding of the Scripture. If we don't need the teaching of others, why do we need theirs?

Some useful types of reference books are discussed below. (A more complete list of reference books available is included in the appendix, along with some observations about many of them.)

A word study: Use word studies like those of *Wuest* or *Vine*. They give you the cultural background, tying it in with history and geography. Write down any significant facts you find. (You church librarian or Christian bookstore owner will be happy to introduce you to these books.)

An atlas: From a word study book, you could go to a Bible atlas. If you are studying John 4 where it says they had to leave Judea to go into Galilee by passing through Samaria, get out a map. Where is it? At this point you may want to draw a map. Here was Judea, here was Galilee. Here was Samaria in between. Maybe record some points of significance from the atlas. Write out anything you observe that will be of help.

An atlas is essential; sometimes, it is the key to unlocking your understanding of a passage. For example, you cannot study the book of Joshua without a map. The map gives you Joshua's unique battle strategy in defeating the enemies in the land, strategy copied even today. General MacArthur admired General Joshua. He studied Joshua's battle strategy. So did Moshe Dayan.

To understand the significance of Christ's ministry, it is essential that we understand where He traveled. To study Paul, his character and his hardships, is to study a map of the terrain in which he traveled.

Encyclopedias and commentaries: After the atlas, go to biblical commentaries and encyclopedias. However, do not hesitate to check out the *Encyclopedia Brittanica*. It is very good in many situations. Biblical commentaries can be very helpful.

LOOKING CLOSER TO HOME

- TOPICAL BOOKS

Books on individual subjects like justification, redemption, salvation, and sanctification are available. Read those in the area you are studying. If you are studying the Holy Spirit, check those books on the Holy Spirit. Write down anything of significance.

Through reading and studying appropriate books, you can understand the historical and cultural background of a passage or word so much better and this is *so important*. Discover what the times were like when Nehemiah lived, for instance. Nehemiah was a cupbearer—was that an important position? The only way to gain a good understanding of the importance of a cupbearer is to read encyclopedias and commentaries. Yes, it is worth it! A great wealth of information has been recorded for us through the labors of many authors and researchers.

We do not interpret the words and meanings of a portion of Scripture in the 20th century without reference to their historical and cultural setting. For example, many people say that Jesus never really claimed to be God. Well, if that is the case, the Pharisees sure got the wrong impression. John 10:33 clearly points out that the Jews sought to stone Jesus because He made Himself out to be God. The question is not what do *I* think, but what did *they* think in their particular circumstances and time.

Once you have gone through all these steps, you will come up with some fantastic information. You started with the Bible, and then you went to what other men and women have taught through the gifts God has given them. We gain from their knowledge and research by using their books and tapes.

But please notice, in the method we are learning, that we start with the Bible and *then* go to other books. I am the first to admit that we can depend too much on books and related Bible study helps, just as we can depend too much on our pastor or Bible teacher for scriptural knowledge. We need to dig into God's Word personally.

▼ STEP FOUR ▼
KNOW YOUR BIBLE

● SUMMARY AND OUTLINE

Now, you have all this material, and you probably have used several sheets of paper. What do you think the next step is? That's right! Outline it—put it in order. Do you know why you need to outline it? You may have something on culture on pages 1, 2, and 5, while definitions are on pages 2 and 4. Get the picture? Your notes and charts are a hodge-podge from all your research. But if you organize all that information under specific headings, it will enable you to (1) learn your material more effectively and (2) teach it with greater clarity. Without the outline, both will be difficult.

A *hint:* Bible dictionaries often give *excellent* outlines for arranging your material. And there is nothing wrong with using one of those outlines. But first try to be creative yourself.

Take the word *Pharisee.* You might have an Old Testament usage, a New Testament usage, a historical meaning, how to become a Pharisee, who was a Pharisee, and so on. You take all your material and fit it into an outline, using those headings. It will be of much greater value and use to you.

Let me show you an outline. You have several in the appendix. The one we'll look at here is on John 3:5 where I did a cross-reference study on "water." I did not have time to do all the steps of interpretation, so I just outlined the cross-reference chart. I had all the cross-reference verses and all their points of significance. How could I teach the passage? I had to outline it. So what did I do? I went back and found four basic divisions: (1) water, (2) water as the Word, (3) water as the Spirit, and (4) water with reference to being born again. So, I took all my cross-references and put them in an outline under the headings Water, Word, Spirit and Born Again. All I did was rearrange my cross-reference chart into a logical organization so that I could study it and teach it more effectively.

LOOKING CLOSER TO HOME

INTERPRETATION OUTLINE OF "WATER"

I.   Water

    A.   Symbolic — not always literal
       1.   Word (Ephesians 5:26)
       2.   Eternal life (John 4:14, 7:36-39)
       3.   Holy Spirit (John 7:39)

    B.   Use of water: Washing (Ephesians 5:26; Hebrews 10:22)

II. Word

    A.   Symbolic
       1.   Seed (1 John 3:9)
       2.   Sword of the Spirit (Ephesians 6:17)

    B.   Use
       1.   Cleanse (Ephesians 5:26; John 15:3; Psalm 119:9,10)
       2.   Sanctify (John 17:17; 1 Peter 1:2; 1 Corinthians 6:11)
       3.   Quickeneth (Psalm 119:50; Hebrews 4:12)
       4.   Work in believer (1 Thessalonians 2:13)

III. Spirit

    A.   Quickens (John 6:26)

    B.   Sanctifies (1 Peter 1:2)
       The agent is the Word (John 17:17; 1 Corinthians 6:11)

    C.   Gives life (John 6:63)

IV. Born again

    A.   Water (John 3:5)

    B.   Spirit (John 3:5)

    C.   Word (1 Corinthians 4:15; James 1:18; 1 Peter 1:23; John 1:13; James 1:15)

    D.   Seed (1 Peter 1:23; 1 John 3:9)

(See pages 164-179 for more samples.)

On pages 123-131 there is also a more detailed guide to outlining, with examples, for the student with more time. Look at the outline of John 4 on worship (p. 169). This is where all the steps of interpretation were done. Actually, I think I used a Bible dictionary's outline for my own. I took all the material that I had gathered from the cross-reference and the other steps of interpretation and put it into a logical sequence. Why? When I go to study it myself or teach it, I have everything together. I do not have to jump from one page to another. It is right there. I can file it away, and five years from now I can take it out and it will still make sense to me.

Remember, this is your Bible study method. Therefore, the observations recorded and the amount of detail in your outline will be determined by the purpose of your study and the time you have.

To review this again, let's go all the way back to the book chart. We begin with chapter titles. These are "handles" to help us grasp and recall the basic content of each chapter.

From the chapter titles, we go to the paragraph titles.

Then, we go to the steps of observation. We have the observation chart with three columns: on the left, the Scripture; in the center column, the observations we have made; and on the right, our questions for interpretation.

The next step is answering the questions of interpretation. The first thing to do in interpretation is the cross-reference study. A cross-reference chart has the cross-reference sources on the left, and the point of significance on the right. You start looking up cross-references. In John 3:1, you go to Luke 23:13, and so on.

From the cross-reference study you go to the interpretation. That is where you write out at the top of a piece of paper what you want to interpret. You start out with the context, the verses both before and after, and write out any significance you gain from context.

▼ STEP FOUR ▼
LOOKING CLOSER TO HOME

The next step is to check out versions, paraphrases, and translations of the text. Then, you go to the dictionaries for definitions. You begin with a secular dictionary and then go to a Bible dictionary. After these sources, go to other Bible study helps such as atlases, encyclopedias, word studies, and individual books on the subject under investigation. Do not forget to document your sources. The final step of interpretation is the organizing, or outlining, of all the material you have gathered.

Remember, the best commentary on the Bible is the Bible. Isn't that amazing? If God is the greatest author, why not have Him as the best commentator? Scripture interprets itself. That is one reason I believe it is important not to skip over the cross-reference step.

Now the "rubber meets the road" as we move to application.

Assignment

1. Take a key word from John 9 and define it.
2. Read a portion of John 9 in two translations and a paraphrase and record your findings.
3. Find an encyclopedia or commentary and see what light it can shed on the historical understanding of the above word or passage.

Application "Do It"

CHAPTER NINE

Where the Rubber Hits the Road

Did I firmly believe as millions say they do that the knowledge and practice of religion would mean to me everything, I would cast away earthly enjoyments as dross, earthly cares as follies, and earthly thoughts and feelings as vanity. Religion would be my first waking thought, and my last image before sleep sank me into unconsciousness. I should labor in its cause alone. I would take thought for the morrow of eternity alone. I would esteem one soul gained for heaven worth a life of suffering. Earthly consequences should never stay my hand, nor seal my lips. Earth, its joys and griefs, would occupy no moment of my thoughts. I would strive to look upon eternity alone, and on the immortal souls around me, soon to be everlastingly miserable. I would go forth to the world and preach to it in season and out of season, and my text would be, "What shall it profit a man if he gain the whole world and lose his own soul?"

— an atheist's statement

This statement of a young atheist had a profound effect on a great British missionary from Cambridge University, C. T. Studd, who later went on to claim, "If Christ be God and died for me, then there is nothing too great I can do for Him." What is it that drove men like him? What motivated men like reformer John Knox, who fell to his knees and cried, "O God, give me Scotland or I die!" One thinks of Jon Huss, the Bohemian reformer who was burned at the stake, or the great Englishman, John Wycliffe, martyred for his faith as he sought to translate the Word of God into the language of the people.

▼ STEP FIVE ▼
WHERE THE RUBBER HITS THE ROAD

What was it that drove these men on in the cause of Christ? Where did they cast their anchor in such perilous times when their very lives were in jeopardy? Martin Luther stood before the emperor in the Cathedral at Worms and was commanded to recant his heretical view of salvation by grace alone. But Luther faced the emperor and boldly asserted, "I cannot recant. My conscience is held captive to *the Word of God"* (emphasis added).

Jesus Christ urged us to build our lives on His Word. Matthew 7:24-27 says:

> Therefore every one who hears these words of Mine, and acts upon them, may be compared to a wise man, who built his house upon the rock. And the rain descended, and the floods came, and the winds blew, and burst against that house; and yet it did not fall, for it had been founded upon the rock. And everyone who hears these words of Mine, and does not act upon them, will be like a foolish man, who built his house upon the sand. And the rain descended, and the floods came, and the winds blew, and burst against that house; and it fell, and great was its fall.

One of the Lord's points was that the one who acts on His Words will have a permanent source of stability. Christ wants us to have that stability in our lives.

He wants us to grow more than even we want to grow. Often we get bogged down in application and feel guilty because we either do not make any specific application for change or we have got so many things we can apply that we do not know where to begin. Therefore, we end up by not applying anything.

Yet Christ does not want us to feel guilty. He realizes (even though sometimes we fail to see it) that we cannot be mature overnight. Growth takes time. We need not only dependence on the Lord, but also a commitment. Look at Galatians 2:20: "I have been crucified with Christ; and it is no longer I who live, but Christ lives in me; and the life which I now live in the flesh I live by faith in the Son of God, who loved me, and delivered Himself up for me." Often we look at just the first part of the verse, which focuses on "It is no longer I who live." Yet that is not Paul's point; rather, it introduces his main point. Notice the second half. It is not only "Christ lives in me"—that is the *Lord's* work—but *also* "the life which I now live ....[is] by faith in the Son of God." That is *our* part.

Application does not mean that we immediately apply everything we learn. Rather, it means we apply all we can. For some, that may be a small amount. Others may have a larger capacity. The Lord will help us, even if it means taking small steps, one at a time. He is as much concerned with the process as He is with the end product.

One problem in the Christian life is that we are often satisfied with interpretation and never get to application. But remember that the goal of Bible study is not interpretation, but application.

●   SIX BASIC QUESTIONS

The following six questions ought to be asked of the truths you have discovered in the passage you are studying. They are basic to helping you apply to your life the material you found through observation and interpretation. What I do is take a sheet of paper and title it "Application." I have before me the Scripture verses, the observation charts and the outline of the interpretation material.

The first thing I do is write down what the basic truths are in a portion of Scripture. Usually, I try to find at least four or five basic truths, or principles, that are taught.

The number of truths you find will be according to your time or your purpose. If you are going to be teaching five hours on John 3:1-10, for example, you had better find ten basic truths, and you will need to spend a lot of time in research and study. Usually, you will come up with three to five principles in a particular passage. But one of the students taking a course from me in Bible study methods recorded 36 basic truths from John 3:1-8 (see p. 180). After listing the basic truths in a passage, I then ask the following six questions of each truth:

WHERE THE RUBBER HITS THE ROAD

1. How does this truth apply to my life (at work? in my neighborhood? at home? in my nation? etc.)? Write out in detail.

2. In view of this truth, what specific changes should I make in my life? List several.

3. How do I propose to carry out these changes? In determining this, you must be specific. I remember when I was studying worship. I was applying basic truths from John 4 and had done my outline on worship. I used as one of my basic truths: Worship God in spirit and truth. I found out as I studied (worship) that when you help other people in Christ's name, you are actually worshipping God. The one truth there was to minister to others.

I asked myself the question, "How do I propose to make this change?" I determined to be more willing to help people, I would go out of my way to assist people as Jesus did in John 4.

At that time, I was living in the mountains above San Bernardino, California, teaching at the Institute of Biblical Studies at Arrowhead Springs. In the summertime in the mountains, there are always people along the side of the road with overheated cars, in esperate need of water. So I bought two big 5-gallon gasoline cans, filled them with water, and carried them in the back of my car. When I left to go home each day, I made sure I had an extra half hour to go up the mountain. If I saw people with their car boiling over, I stopped and offered them some water.

After I would fill up their radiator, they would almost always say, "Let me pay you." Almost always! But I would say, "No, but could I have several minutes of your time?" And I would share the Four Spiritual Laws with them. In this way, I found out I was worshipping God in giving water to the people who needed it going up the mountain. Plus, I was able to use the situation to share the "Good News."

How did I propose to carry out these truths? Get large containers and fill them with water!

4. What is my personal prayer regarding this truth? I think you should write out that personal prayer. Lay it right out on the table, before you and the Lord. *Prayer personalizes the principle*.

5. What verse (or verses) of Scripture would I memorize to best summarize this truth?

6. What illustration can I develop that will help me to retain this truth and communicate it to others? You might incorporate a graphic, a cartoon, a drawing, a story, or a poem.

Here is a sample application step by a student using these questions:

APPLICATION

Ephesians 4:11-16

1. *Application*. If each Christian maximizes his or her spiritual gift, and works to serve the body in love, the Great Commission could be fulfilled by 1990. Therefore, in love, I will seek to motivate my brothers and sisters to find, develop, and use their spiritual gifts.

2. *Changes*. My efforts could be concentrated, strategically, in my local church, in Campus Crusade for Christ or in some other Christian service organization. I should spend more time applying my management skills to my assignments.

3. *Carry out*. Increase my reading and studying to include more books on management. Seek to simplify the registration process to build the effectiveness of the Christian conference. Spend time documenting my research for others in the body.

4. *Personal prayer*. Lord, may I use my spiritual gift of administration to build up the body of Christ. May the body grow in love as I use my gift to help fulfill the Great Commission.

5. *Verse.* Verse 16.

6. *Illustration.* Body of Christ:

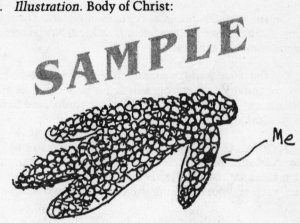

(See pages 181-185 for more samples.)

• SOME THINGS TO CONSIDER

People ask, "Why, is this section on application so short, especially if application is the most important part of Bible study?"

Contrary to what most people think, the most important part is not necessarily the longest. In fact, in our culture, we cater to that erroneous idea. We would rather read a *long chapter* on "How to Apply God's Word," or even a whole book on the subject, because it makes us feel good! By reading it, we often fool ourselves into believing we have applied it.

The main reason this section is shorter than the rest is that the bulk of the work for application takes place in observation and interpretation, especially in observation. The more you see, the more you will understand *and* the easier it will be to understand. And understanding facilitates application.

There are basically two types of applications we make from the Word, those that come easily and are on the "surface," and those for which we must dig.

On the surface we can make easy application of "Don't commit adultery." No shades of gray here. No searching for strong personal application.

On the other hand, a passage like 1 Peter 1:14-16 is clear, but one must think and dig a little for how it can be applied. What does "holy" mean? Or how does "conformed to the former lusts" apply to me? To my lifestyle?

And then there are truths that come as a result of keen observation. These are not explicitly stated and can include such ideas as: How did Jesus disciple His men? What was Paul's strategy for fulfilling the Great Commission?

Your success in the area of application will depend for the most part on the effort you put forth to answer the above six questions and your trust in the Holy Spirit to make God's truths a reality in your experience.

The next section deals with ways that you can be side-tracked in the step of application

● SANDTRAPS TO SIDESTEP

When a golfer tees off, he whacks his ball straight for the pin. In his attempt for a hole-in-one, he faces many hazards that would love to swallow his ball — water traps on one side and sand traps on the other. All are obstacles to the golfer.

Application in Bible study has similar hazards. There are various traps that we occasionally land in during our growth process through Bible study.

Yet, we do not need to take up permanent residence in them if we are aware of what they are. Let's face it, Satan would like nothing better than to short-circuit our attempt to get into God's Word on a more consistent and structured basis.

WHERE THE RUBBER HITS THE ROAD

The first hazard is the practice of *mistaking interpretation for application*. We sometimes assume that because we have understood something, therefore we have applied it. For example, we know that practicing good hospitality is scriptural. Thus, we may assume we are hospitable in what we do, since we understand this truth. In actuality, that may not be true at all. As growing Christians, we often learn a great deal, and it is easy to assume we have translated our knowledge into experience.

Another obstacle can be *procrastination*. So often we do not feel like studying the Bible. This is to be expected. After all, especially if you are a fairly new believer, you are trying to establish new habit patterns of obeying God after years of operating in the flesh or running on your emotions. Strong and consistent desires must be built over time; old desires and habits do not fall away easily. The question becomes, "Will we let our feelings rule us and procrastinate, or will we take up arms against it?"

As we attempt to grow and apply the truth, we are fighting a battle with the flesh (Romans 7). The Lord calls us to realize that the battle is won (Romans 6 and 8). We are conquerors through Christ and can do all things through Him who strengthens us (Romans 8 and Philippians 4).

We can press on. With procrastination we are talking of priorities. For whenever you put one thing off until later, you always do something else now. It is a question of what we will do whether we feel like it or not.

Often I don't feel like studying God's Word. But what motivates me to spend time in the Scriptures is not my emotions; rather, it is my *convictions*. My deep belief that "God has spoken" supercedes my feelings.

A third obstacle that short-circuits our application is an *emotional response*. We get caught up with some truth the Lord may have shown us. Our response may be one of heightened joy or the godly sorrow of a broken heart. Yet that genuine emotion does not move over into the area of action.

A fourth hazard to look out for, especially in our culture, is that of trying to achieve *instant results*. We so often want to have those new areas of our life that need work brought under control or changed by yesterday. We fail to realize that the Lord is just as interested in the process as He is in the product. For it is usually by the process that we grow. Faith is developed over time and through knowledge.

The final obstacle is *frustration*. We wonder, "Will this, if I apply it, really make a difference in my life?" Yes, of course it will. God promises that His Word causes growth and helps us to develop the mind of Christ. This truth relates to the previous area of trusting God through the process, through the crucible of life in which He purifies our character and molds our thinking.

All of us occasionally land in the "sandtraps." What is important is that we blast out as soon as we can and try to steer clear of them. The Lord is not as concerned that we may end up in a trap as He is with what we do once we find ourselves there. For the growth process builds character, and part of this is the process of walking through the obstacles. No one hits a hole-in-one consistently. It takes two to three shots to reach the hole (for some of us seven or eight). And it takes time to develop a good game. The point is to stick with it.

Assignment

1. Ask the six application questions of your study of John 9.
2. Set a definite time to apply one of the truths learned to your life and situation.

▼ *C H A P T E R   T E N* ▼

Crisis Bible Study

Every day we face crisis: emotional, physical, marital, economic, and so on. We are in a constant need of knowing God's will or seeing His perspective on different situations. So many Christians' lives are like "rally coasters." They rally and then they coast, up and down. One minute they are on top of it, and the next minute defeated. One day they are joyful, and the next day they are disheartened.

The questions I often hear are: "How can I best deal with crisis situations?" "What can I do about the 'ups and downs' of my walk with Christ?"

For me, the saturation of my mind with the Word of God and the application of it to my life is the beginning of stability. An extensive knowledge of the Scripture is an effective foundation for facing crisis. Paul said that "faith comes from hearing, and hearing by the word of Christ" (Romans 10:17). The more we fill our minds and thoughts with God's perspective on situations, the more our lives will take on stability. Our knowledge of the Bible becomes a reservoir of help for handling crisis situations. This is one of the reasons I wrote this *Guide to Understanding Your Bible.* I want to give you, the reader, simple steps to help you gain a greater understanding of God's Word.

KNOW YOUR BIBLE

For many readers, however, it will take a while, even with this approach, to acquire an extensive knowledge of Scripture. Therefore, I have included this chapter on "Crisis Bible Study" as a stop gap. It is designed to help those who as yet do not have a working knowledge of the Word to be better able to deal with difficult situations as they develop.

The first source of help is a categorized list of scriptural references that will help you to find passages that apply to your area of hurt or need. You will find this list, entitled "Topical Index for Crisis Bible Study," at the end of the chapter. As you see that God knows and cares how you feel, it will give you hope and courage. One cry of the psalmist is that God cares (Psalms 23, 56, 121).

The Scripture verses will help you see what God has to say about your problem, frustration, or decision to be made. It is my conviction that when a Christian sees what the Bible says, it is easier to adjust or correct his thoughts or actions. This is especially true of those who have a heart that is sensitive to God.

Waylon Ward, a Dallas counselor, explains why he believes in the use of Scripture in counseling and crisis situations:

> As a Christian who takes the Bible very seriously, I have always believed in its authority. However, when I began to use it in counseling, I became convinced of its power. There is a power in the Word of God that transforms lives (Isa. 55:11). When a person meditates on and studies a passage of Scripture that applies to his problem, dramatic results often occur. Often these results can be explained only as the supernatural working of the Holy Spirit. The Spirit takes the Word of God and uses it to heal the pain the person feels. This transforming power which leads to a renewing of the mind is definitely a unique aspect of Christian counseling. (Waylon Ward, *The Bible In Counseling*, Chicago, IL; Moody Press, 1977, p.18)

The second source of help I want to introduce you to is the tremendous book by Waylon Ward referred to above. It contains 40 studies that are indexed to more than 15 topics. Each study leads a person toward an emotional understanding and application of God's Word. Each focuses a person's attention on God's love, grace, and acceptance. Not only are the various lessons biblically based, but they are also psychologically sound.

When a person purchases a copy of *The Bible in Counseling*, he also obtains the rights to reproduce the individual studies for use in his own ministry. The pages are designed to be torn from the book for easy duplication. This tool will not only help you personally, but will also be a valuable asset in helping others who have certain needs or are facing a particular crisis.

The two examples that follow will give you a feel for the types of personal studies available in *The Bible in Counseling*.

STUDY GUIDE TO PSALM 40:1-3

(depression, hopelessness, despair)

Read the verses from two or three different versions and a paraphrase. Particularly recommended are the *New American Standard Bible* and *The Living Bible*.

1. What two things did the psalmist do in these verses?
   a. *Waited for the Lord.*
   b. *Cried unto the Lord.*

2. What six things did the Lord do for the psalmist?
   a. *Turned to him.*
   b. *Heard his cry.*
   c. *Lifted him out of the slimy pit*
   d. *Set his feet on a rock*
   e. *Gave him a firm place to stand.*
   f. *Put a new song in his mouth.*

3. Where did the new song come from? *From the Lord.*

4. What was the old song? *His crying and tears.*

5. What will be the results of the Lord doing these things for the psalmist? (v. 3)
   Many will see what God has done and trust in Him

6. What is your "pit of destruction" or "miry clay"? *My grief and depression.*

7. What are you doing about your situation? *I have been crying to God -- and trying to wait on the Lord.*

   Are you doing what the psalmist did? *Yes*

8. What can you expect the Lord to do for you because He did it for the psalmist?
   The same things -- pick me up -- set me on firm ground -- give me a new song.

9. What is going to result from your situation as it did from the psalmist's situation?
   People will see and hear what God has done.

10. On the basis of what God is going to do for you, what should be your attitude?
    (See also Rom 8:28 and 1 Thess 5:18.) *I can praise Him and thank Him that He will work through my pain (Psalm 119:71)*

11. When can you expect God to do this work in your life? *I don't know when -- I hope soon (1 Peter 5:10 - "a little while*

12. Write these three verses on small cards and place them around where you work or live so you can meditate on them throughout the day, every day!

STUDY GUIDE TO 2 CORINTHIANS 12:7-10

(trials, weaknesses, problems)

Read 2 Corinthians 12:1-10 from two or three different versions and a paraphrase. Recommended are the *New American Standard Bible* and *The Living Bible*. After you have read these ten verses a few times, begin to concentrate your thoughts on verses 7-10.

Write a one-sentence summary of these three verses: *When I feel weak, God will strengthen me; God's grace is sufficient for my weaknesses.*

Answer the following questions:

1. Why was Paul given this thorn in the flesh? (v. 7) *To keep him from being conceited.*

2. What do you think Paul's "thorn" was? *Possibly eyes were bad.*

   Why do you believe it was that? *I heard it taught once.*

   Does it say in the passage what Paul's "thorn" was? *No*

3. Why do you think that God did not tell us what Paul's "thorn" was? *So I can identify with the truth of these verses.*

4. Do you have a "thorn in the flesh" that continually seems to defeat you? *Yes*

   What is your personal thorn? *Lack of self-confidence and inferiority feelings.*

5. Is it possible that Paul's "thorn" was similar to your thorn in the flesh? *I guess so.*

6. What did Paul do about his "thorn"? *He asked God three times to remove it.*

   Have you done the same about yours? *I have asked Him to heal me of these feelings.*

7. Could God have removed Paul's "thorn" if He desired to do so? *Yes.*

   Why did God not remove Paul's "thorn"? *So he could learn to trust God more and not depend on himself.*

8. Does God possibly have a reason for not removing your personal "thorn"? *Yes -- I think He did.*

What do you believe is His reason in your case? *To keep me dependent on Him.*

9. God told Paul, "My *grace* is *sufficient* for you." (v. 9). Would He tell you something different? *No.*

10. Where is God's power perfected? *In weakness -- specifically in my weakness.*

11. What does Paul gladly do then? *He delights in insults, weaknesses, hardships, persecutions and difficulties.*

Why? *Because when he is weak, he is strong with God's strength*

12. Paul says he is *Content/delighted* (v. 10) with five things. What are they?

    a. *weaknesses*

    b. *insults*

    c. *hardships*

    d. *persecutions*

    e. *difficulties*

13. What should be your attitude about your "thorn" in the flesh? *I should delight in it because it keeps me dependent on my heavenly Father.*

14. This passage teaches us strength is given for weakness; not in spite of our weakness, but because of it. It is weakness that qualifies a man for divine strength. Are you qualified? *Most definitely*

15. Grace is the catalyst that transforms every failure, every sin, every defeat, every imperfection and exploits them for spiritual growth and maturity. Does Romans 8:28 include your thorn in the flesh? *Yes! God can (and has) use my thorn for His glory.*

16. Read 1 Corinthians 15:10, "By the *grace* [not *mistake*] of God I am, what I am" (from the *New American Standard Bible*).

17. What should be your attitude toward your "thorn" or any problem in your life? (1 Thess 5:18) *An attitude of thanksgiving and acceptance.*

CRISIS BIBLE STUDY

**TOPICAL INDEX
FOR CRISIS BIBLE STUDY**

Problem	Study Guide
Affection Needs	Acts 27
Alcohol and Drugs	Gen. 1:28
	Num. 6:2-4
	Deut. 6:4
	Ps. 55:22
	104
	Prov. 20:1
	23:20
	23:29-35
	31:4-6
	Isa. 5:11
	Matt. 11:19
	16:27-29
	27:34
	Mark 15:23
	Luke 7:33, 34
	10:34
	John 2:9, 10
	14:6
	Rom. 12:1
	13:1-5
	13:13
	14:21
	1 Cor. 5:11
	6:10-12
	6:19, 20
	Gal. 5:16-21
	Eph. 5:18
	Col. 3:2
	1 Tim. 2:5
	5:23
	1 Thes. 5:4-8
	1 Pet. 1:13
	2:13-17
	4:3, 4
	5:7
	Rev. 9:20, 21
	18:23
	21:8
	22:15

Problem	Study Guide
Anger	Almost 600 references to Anger or Wrath in the Bible
	Ps. 2:5-9
	7:11
	10
	95:11
	130:3, 4
	Isa. 48:9
	Dan. 9:9
	Amos 5:18-20
	Nah. 1:2, 3
	1:6-8
	Mark 3:5
	Rom. 1:18
	2:5
	1 Thes. 1:10
	2:1b
	2 Pet. 3:9
	Rev. 6

Warning Against Human Anger
Ps. 37:8
Prov. 10:18
14:17, 29
15:1, 18
16:32
20:3, 22
22:24, 25
24:29
26:24
27:5, 6
29:11, 20, 22
Eccl. 7:9
Matt. 5:22
7:1-5
Luke 17:3, 4
Rom. 12:19
14:4
2 Cor. 7:8-10
Gal. 5:20
Eph. 4:26-32
Col. 3:8
2 Tim. 4:2
Heb. 12:15

(Cont'd)

(Cont'd)

Problem	Study Guide	Problem	Study Guide
	James 1:19, 20		Phil. 4:4-9
	3:3-14		Heb. 13:6
	4:1		James 1:22
	5:9		1 John 4:18
	Dealing With It	Death	Ps. 23:6
	Gen. 4:5-7		Prov. 3:21-26
	Prov. 15:28		14:32
	19:19		1 Cor. 15:54-58
	22:24, 25		Phil. 1:21, 23
	25:15		Heb. 2:14, 15
	Matt. 6:12	Decision	2 Tim. 3:15-18
	18:21, 22	Making	Heb. 11:23-27
	18:33-35	Depression	(Despair)
	Gal. 5:18-25		Gen. 4:6, 7
	Eph. 4:15		Ex. 6:9
	Phil. 4:4-11		Num. 11:10-15
	James 5:16		1 Kings 19
	1 Pet. 1:13		Job 3
	2:23		Ps. 23:4
	1 John 1:9		27
	Causes		32
	Matt. 2:16		34:15-17
	Mark 10:14		38
	John 4		40:1-3
	Effects		51
	Ps. 73		69
	Prov. 14:17		88
	25:28		102
	Matt. 5:38;44		103:13, 14
	Eph. 4:30, 31		121
Anxiety	Bad		Prov. 18:14
	Ps. 55:22		Lamentations
	121		Matt. 5:12
	Matt. 6:25-34		11:28-30
	Acts 27		26:37, 38
	Phil. 4:6, 7		26:75
	1 Pet. 5:7		John 4:1-3
	Good		15:10, 11
	2 Cor. 11:28		Acts 27
	Phil. 2:20		Rom. 8:28
	"Cures"—		15:13
	Dealing With It		2 Cor. 4:8, 9
	John 14:1-3		Eph. 1:3-14
	14:18, 27		Dealing With It
			John 14:1-4
			14:26, 27

▼ S T E P F I V E ▼
CRISIS BIBLE STUDY

Problem	Study Guide	Problem	Study Guide
	Col 1:16, 17		Matt. 5:2
	Heb. 1:3		5:27, 28
	13:5		5:31, 32
			6:14, 15
	Preventing It		19:3-9
	Phil. 4:11-13		Mark 10:2-12
	Phil. 4:8 – key		Rom. 6:1-2
Desire	Gen. 3:6		12:1-2
	Ex. 20:17		13:14
	Prov. 10:3, 24		1 Cor. 7:10-24
	11:6		7:33-34
	28:25		7:39-40
	Matt. 6:21		Jas. 5:16
	Luke 12:31-34		Causes of
	Rom. 13:14		1 Cor. 7:10-15
	Gal. 5:16		Preventing
	Eph. 2:3		1 Sam. 12:33
	Titus 2:12	Endurance	Ps. 40:1-3
	3:3		John 11
	Jas. 1:13-16		Acts 27
	4:2, 3		2 Cor. 12:7-10
	1 John 2:16		Heb. 12:5-11
	Jude 18	Envy	Titus 3:3
	1 Pet. 1:14		Jas. 3:14-16
	4:2, 3		1 Pet. 2:1
Discipline	Prov. 3:11, 12	Fear	Gen. 3:10
	13:24		Ps. 103
	19:18		121
	22:6, 15		Prov. 10:24
	23:13		29:25
	29:15		Matt. 10:26-31
	1 Cor. 5:1-13		Acts 27
	11:29-34		2 Tim. 1:7
	2 Cor. 2:1-11		Heb. 2:14, 15
	12:7-10		1 Pet. 3:6
	Eph. 6:1-4		3:13, 14
	1 Tim. 4:7		1 John 4:18
	Heb. 12:5-11	Financial	Deut. 8:11-14
Divorce	Gen. 2:18-25		Job 31:24-25
	Ex. 20:14		31:28
	Deut. 24:1-4		Ps. 49:10-12
	Isa. 50:1		52:5-7
	Jer. 3:1		62:10
	Mal. 2:16		

(Cont'd)

Problem	Study Guide	Problem	Study Guide
	Prov. 3:9		Rom. 18:8, 9
	10:9		Gal. 6:10
	11:1		1 Thes. 3:10
	15:27		Rev. 3:17
	17:23		**Dealing With**
	19:17		Gen. 1:28
	22:7		Ex. 20:15, 27
	23:4, 5		Ps. 50:10-12
	27:24		50:15
	28:20		55:22
	30:7-10		Matt. 6:25-34
	Eccl. 5:10		25:14-29
	Matt. 6:24-34		1 Pet. 5:7
	18:23-25	Forgiveness	Ps. 32
	19:16-24		103
	25:14-30		Prov. 17:9
	Mark 6:7-11		Matt. 6:14, 15
	8:36		18:15-17
	Luke 12:13-21		Mark 11:25
	16:19f		Luke 17:3-10
	Rom. 13:6-8		Eph. 4:32
	1 Cor. 16:2		Col. 3:13
	2 Cor. 8:14, 15		Jas. 5:15
	9:7		1 John 1:8-10
	Phil. 4:18, 19	Friendship	Prov. 27:6, 10
	1 Tim. 6:7, 10		17:9, 17
	Heb. 13:5		John 15:13-15
	Causes of	God's Love &	Ps. 27
	Ex. 20:17	Acceptance	103
	Ps. 72:2, 3		Luke 15
	Prov. 3:9-10		Acts 27
	3:27-28	Gossip	Prov. 10:18
	11:15		11:13
	11:24, 25		18:8
	14:21		20:19
	17:18		26:20-22
	19:15, 17		Jas. 4:11
	21:5	Grief	2 Sam. 12
	22:7		Ps. 6:5-7
	22:26, 27		23:4
	28: 20, 22		119:28
	Eccl. 5:15-17		137:1, 5, 6
	Mal. 8:10		Prov. 14:13
	Luke 3:11		15:13
	6:38		
	12:15-21		

CRISIS BIBLE STUDY

Problem	Study Guide	Problem	Study Guide
	Matt. 5:4		1 Peter 3:18
	14:12-21		1 John 1:8, 9
	26:38		Preventing
	John 11		Eph. 4:32
	1 Cor. 15	Habit	Prov. 19:19
	2 Cor. 4:14-5:8		Isa. 1:10-17
	Eph. 4:30		Jer. 13:23
	1 Thes. 4		22:21
	2 Tim. 1:10		Rom. 6-7
	Heb. 2:14, 15		Gal. 5:16-21
	9:27		1 Tim.
Guilt	Ps. 32		Heb. 5:13ff.
	103		1 Pet. 2:14, 19
	Isa. 53:6	Homo-	Gen. 19
	Matt. 6:12	sexuality	Lev. 18:22
	18:21f		20:13
	Luke 15		Rom. 1:26-32
	Rom. 8:23		1 Cor. 6:9-11
	2 Cor. 7:8-10		1 Tim. 1:10
	1 Pet. 1:24	Hope	Ps. 27
	1 John 1:9		40:1-3
	Causes		119
	Gen. 2:17		121
	3:4, 5		Prov. 10:28
	3:8, 22		13:12
	Job 1:9-11		Acts 27
	John 14:26		Rom. 15:4, 5
	16:8, 13		1 Thes. 1:3
	Rom. 2:18		4:13-18
	1 Cor. 8:10-12		Heb. 6:11, 18-19
	10:28, 29	Hopelessness,	Ps. 27
	Phil. 3:12-16	Despair	40:1-3
	1 Tim. 4:2		103
	1 John 1:8-10		121
	Rev. 12:10		John 11
	Effects		Acts 27
	Ps. 73	Humility	Prov. 13:34
	Rom. 6:23		15:33
	1 John 1:9		16:19
	Dealing With It		22:4
	1 Sam. 16:7		29:23
	Ps. 103:14		John 13:1-17
	139:1-4		Gal. 6:1, 2
	John 8:3-11		
	James 5:16		(Cont'd)

(Cont'd)

Problem	Study Guide	Problem	Study Guide
	Eph. 5:15-21	Lying	Ex. 20:16
	Phil. 2:1-11		Prov. 12:19, 22
	Jas. 4:6, 10		Eph. 4:25
	1 Pet. 5:6, 7		Col. 3:9
Laziness	Prov. 12:24, 27	Marital	Gen. 2:18-25
	13:4	Problems	Deut. 24:1-4
	15:19		Prov. 5:18
	18:9		8:22
	26:13-16		19:13
	Matt. 25:26		21:9
Life-dominat-	1 Cor. 6:9-12		19
ing Problems	21:8		27:15, 16
	Eph. 5:18		Eccl. 9:9
	Rev. 21:8		Matt. 5:31, 32
	22:15		19:3-9
Loneliness	Gen. 2:18		1 Cor. 7:10-16
	Ps. 25:16		Eph. 5:21-33
	121		Col. 3:18-25
	Luke 15		Heb. 13:4
	John 11		1 Pet. 3:1-7
	Acts 27		
	Eph. 1:3-14		Causes of
	2 Tim. 4:9-12		1 Cor. 7:12-16
			2 Cor. 6:14-16
	Dealing With It		Eph. 5:21-33
	Prov. 18:24		Col. 3:18-25
	John 3:16		1 Pet. 3:1-7
	Rom. 8:9	Marriage	Gen. 2:18, 24
	8:14-17		Eph. 5:22-33
	8:26-31		Col. 3:18-21
	8:35-39		1 Pet. 3:1-17
	1 Cor. 6:19		1 Tim. 2:11-15
	1 John 1:9		
	4:13	Parent/Child	Gen. 2:24
Love	Prov. 10:12		2 Cor. 12:14
	17:19		Eph. 6:1-4
	Matt. 5:44		1 Tim. 3:4, 5
	22:39, 40	Peace	Ps. 40:1-3
	Rom. 13:10		119
	1 Cor. 13		121
	1 Pet. 1:22		Prov. 3:1, 2
	1 John 4:10, 19		16:7
	5:2, 3		John 11
	2 John 5, 6		14:27
			Rom. 5:1
			12:18
			14:19

CRISIS BIBLE STUDY

Problem	Study Guide	Problem	Study Guide
	Phil. 4:6-9		Mark 6:7-13
	Col. 3:15		7:24-30
	Heb. 12:14		9:20-27
Pride	Prov. 8:13		Luke 9:1, 2, 6
	11:2		13:1-5
	13:10		John 9:2, 3
	16:18		Rom. 5:3-5
	18:12		8:28
	21:24		1 Cor. 11:29, 30
	27:1		2 Cor. 2:7-10
	29:23		Heb. 9:27
Repentance	Luke 3:8-14		12:11
	24:47		James 1:2-4
	Acts 3:19		5:14-16
	5:31		1 Pet. 1:5-7
	17:30		
	26:20		Dealing With It
	2 Cor. 7:10		Rom. 11:33
	12:21		1 Cor. 12:25, 26
Resentment	Prov. 26:24-26		Heb. 11:1
	Heb. 12:15		James 5:6
Self-Image	Luke 15		1 John 1:9
	Eph. 2:3-14	Singleness	Gen. 2:18
Sickness	Ps. 119:71		Matt. 19:11, 12
	Matt. 9:2-6		1 Cor. 7:7, 28
	9:18-21		7:32-35
	9:23-26		Heb. 12:15, 16
	10:5-8	Worry	Prov. 12:25
	13:58		14:30
	25:39, 40		17:22
			Matt. 6:24-34
			Phil. 4:6, 7
			1 Pet. 5:6, 7

▼ CHAPTER ELEVEN ▼

Conclusion

- ## YOU CAN DO IT

So far, we have detailed the principal steps to follow in order to have an effective personal Bible study and you have been through the process at least partially on your own. Now that we have gone through portions of the Gospel of John together in this study, you are ready to tackle other books! In order to do this and grow in your study, some type of plan is needed.

A Plan

Most people cringe at the thought of having a plan, or even worse, a schedule! The whole concept sends paranoia down the spine of the average individual. What most people do not realize is that they are already on some type of schedule, even though it may not be a very good one. What is at stake here is some type of plan to implement what you have learned into a personal Bible study.

Whether it be simple or highly structured, some organization will help you as you study the Bible. It is important to realize that what is good for one person may be terrible for another. Some people get up at 6 A.M. and put in one hour of solid study. Others may take 15-30 minutes before they go to work, or after dinner. Some people can accomplish in half an hour what it may take others over an hour to do. When you are just beginning, it may not be as wise to set aside as much time for your study as someone who has been at it for 10 years. The fact is that you need to find the best plan for you. No plan is any more spiritual than another. Let's face it, it is pretty difficult to get up at the often supposedly spiritual hour of 5:30A.M. if you happen to be a night nurse working the graveyard shift. Do not put yourself under the pile or force yourself into someone else's mold.

In your planning, don't decide only what time you will study, but also decide on the duration. Will it be every day, seven days a week? Maybe you do it best at certain times during the week. Besides as you incorporate this into your life and start to see the exciting fruit of your study of the Bible, you will find yourself doing it whenever you have a spare minute. The best time for you may be when you have some free time during the day, or a block of time at night. Do it then. Often, mothers with newborn children have the most demanding and erratic schedules. There is no routine! If the baby starts crying, a Bible study method is about the last thing on that mother's mind. It is important not to feel guilty. God will give you wisdom on how to sandwich in some time.

The important thing is not so much the quantity of time or, at this point, even the quality of time, but rather the time itself. Simply spend time in the Word. For you see, when someone first begins to play the piano or the trumpet, it is not really the quantity of time (for it takes time to develop the desire and consistency) or even the quality of time that counts. (Have you ever listened to a trumpet player who is just learning how to play? Don't bank on the quality!) It is the consistency that pays off at first.

A Priority

We need to see Bible study as a priority, as we said at the beginning, not because it is something to do, but because the Lord sees it as a priority. Often we consider studying the Word almost as a job reserved for the "professionals." But Bible study should be incorporated into every believer's devotional life. It is the time when the Lord reveals His truth to us and the Holy Spirit gives us wisdom about how to act and how to grow.

▼ STEP FIVE ▼
CONCLUSION

Make no mistake about it — Bible study is work. It is not always exciting. Often God will take us into the desert to see if we are committed to following through (see Deuteronomy 8). The feelings will not always be there. But the results will be there. God will reward those who study and apply His Word. "Those who honor Me I will honor" (1 Samuel 2:30) is just as true today as it was when God said it to Eli.

A Promise

When we plan a certain time for Bible study and are consistent with it, when we give Bible study the priority it deserves, we will reap the promises of God.

Hebrews 4:12 tells us that the Bible can reveal to us our innermost desires: "The Word of God is living and active and sharper than any two-edged sword...able to judge the thoughts and intentions of the heart." Then in 2 Timothy 3:16 we see how understanding the Scriptures helps us control and direct those desires: "All Scripture is inspired by God and profitable for teaching, for reproof, for correction, for training in righteousness." Through regular exposure, God's Word teaches us, trains us and works to conform us to the image of Christ. When the principles laid down in the Bible become a vital part of our lives, we experience real spiritual growth. We have victory over circumstances, and watching God work in our lives *is* exciting.

You can step into Psalm 119 at almost any point and see the importance of God's Word and the blessings that come from paying heed to it. Also, God tells us in Joshua 1:8 that when we keep His Word in our minds constantly, when we meditate on it day and night, we will get in the habit of being obedient to Him. As a result we will be prosperous and successful — maybe not always in material things, but His work will be accomplished in us and that is real success. And God promised it!

▼ *A P P E N D I X* ▼

Additional Bible Study Steps

- ## OUTLINE

When doing the book charts, we went from chapters to paragraphs. And then we jumped over one of the most difficult steps, yet one of the most valuable — outlining the passage. I always ask my class in Bible study methods, "How many of you came to understand the book of John more than at any other time and learned more in a short period by doing this outline?" Almost 90 percent of the hands go up. When you start to do an outline, you begin to see the way the author was thinking. You begin to see the way things tie together and how they relate.

One of the hardest things for most men and women to do is outline. But if you cannot do it, you will have a difficult time understanding and teaching. The better the teacher, usually the better his material is outlined. If you do not have it organized, you are going to be playing holy hopscotch with your own notes. An outline is structure. It helps you to see more clearly.

Suppose you were going to build a house and the contractor gave you two sheets of paper. The first was a list of the material needed, and the second sheet was a blueprint of the house. Now both sheets contain exactly the same thing — the same materials. Yet one is organized, the other is not. In order to build the house the way it was designed, you need more than just the list of materials that go into the home. You need to know how it all fits together. The same is true of the Word.

For example, the book of Ephesians breaks into two major divisions:

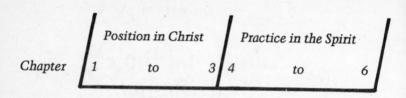

Just to know this is not enough, however. The order or structure is important. The fact that one's position in Christ comes before practice is significant, for as Paul teaches in the book, the one (practice) depends on the understanding of the other (position in Christ).

Outlining comes hard for me, too. I have to struggle with it. But I am so glad that I have put the time in, because now it is starting to come easier. I look forward to it, because I start to comprehend something new every time I do it.

The outline helps you to think through the grammatical and logical relationships of a passage. The first step is to determine the portion of Scripture that you want to outline. Now, if you are outlining an entire book, I would outline each chapter and then go back and put each outline into an overall outline of the book. Instead of trying to do the entire book all at once, first do each chapter.

The points of the outline should develop along the natural development of the passage you seek to outline. Do not try to force something into an outline that is not there in the passage.

In outlining a book or a chapter, use the chapter titles from your charts for the titles of your outline. This way everything in

your outline relates back to the title of the chapter. That makes
it easier! As previously mentioned, when you do a book, do not
feel bound by the chapter divisions. Sometimes, you are going
to find that the last part of one chapter goes better with the next
chapter.

How do you outline? First, find the major divisions in a
chapter. These major divisions are usually the paragraphs. You
can get your paragraph titles from your book chart. As an illustration we shall use John 1:1-18. See page 127. I have four
major points in my outline. The first is "The Word — The Uncreated Creator" (vv. 1-5). For the next, I have "Forerunner of
the Word" (vv. 6-8). The next major division is "Results of the
Word Made Flesh" (vv. 9-13). Then, the fourth major division of
the chapter is "Characteristics of the Word Made Flesh" (vv.
14-18).

Within the major divisions, I try to find minor divisions.
And as you can see in the outline, I have three minor divisions
under the first major one:

I.   The Word — The Uncreated Creator (John 1:1-5)
       A. Eternal existence
       B. Eternal source
       C. Eternal manifestation.

The next step is logical. From each one of those minor divisions, I look to see if those divisions have divisions. In other
words, can the minor divisions be broken up so I can see the sequence of how the chapter develops? For some of them, I could.
"Eternal existence," breaks down into "Divine nature" and
"Since the beginning." Under "Eternal source," I found
"Material world" and "Life." "Eternal manifestation" does not
appear to break down further. Since I can find no division in
that one verse, I leave it alone. Then I go to the next major division, "Forerunner of the Word." I found two minor divisions:

       A. Who? Man sent by God

       B. Purpose

Under *purpose* I found some divisions. I did not find any under the first one.

Then, under my third major division, I found two divisions, one negative and one positive. I considered whether those verses that point out the negative could be broken up and found they could, so I divided them up.

So, I have found that the easiest thing is to find the major divisions and then go back and find the minor divisions. Then I look for still more sub-divisions. You can go on and on.

You start with the larger units and go to the smaller as the next step. Here are some things to be careful of. First, everything under a major division must be included in those verses. Everything in the title must be in the divisions. If you divide up a main point, the new titles must include the content of all the verses. Second, in an outline, never divide a point unless there are two divisions. Never have A without B. Never have "1." without "2.," because the logic is this: If you do not have two divisions, do not divide it. Just put it in the title. If you cannot divide "I." into two separate parts, do not have anything under it. Just leave it "I." Then go to "II.," and if "II." divides, divide it. You see how it goes.

I think as you read through this outline and have it next to John 1, you will start to understand that passage more. I could not believe it when I did this outline. I started to see the progression of it, how it fit together, the grammatical construction, its relationship—things I have never seen before. And I got it through the outline. In addition, when you have an outline, it is a lot easier to teach a particular passage.

ADDITIONAL BIBLE STUDY STEPS

OUTLINE

WITNESS OF THE WORD MADE FLESH (JOHN 1:1-18)

I. The Word — The Uncreated Creator (1-5)
    A. Eternal existence (1-2)
        1. Divine nature (1)
        2. Since the beginning (2)
    B. Eternal source of creation (2-4)
        1. Material world (3)
        2. Life (4)
    C. Eternal manifestation (light) (5)

II. Forerunner of the Word (6-8)
    A. Who? Man sent by God (6)
    B. Purpose? (7-8)
        1. Bear witness of the light (7a, 8)
        2. For all the world to believe (7b)

III. Results of the Word Made Flesh (9-13)
    A. Negative (9-11)
        1. Enlightens every man (9) BUT
        2. Rejected by men (10, 11)
            a. by world (10)
            b. by His own (11)
    B. Positive (12-13)
        1. Children of God by believing (12)
        2. Of God, not man (13)

IV. Characteristics of the Word Made Flesh (14-18)
    A. Only begotten of the Father (14)
    B. Greater rank than forerunner (15)
    C. Channel of grace and truth (16-17)
    D. Visible expression of invisible God (18)

OUTLINE

John 1:1-10

Student Sample

I.   The Word was (John 1:1-4)
    A. In the beginning (John 1:1-2)
    B. With God (John 1:2)
    C. God (John 1:1)
       1. Creator of all things (John 1:3)
       2. In Him was life (John 1:4)
       3. The Life was the light of men (John 1:4)

II.   Light (John 1:5)
    A. Shines in the darkness (John 1:5)
    B. Darkness did not comprehend it (John 1:5)

III.   A man (John 1:6-8)
    A. Sent by God (John 1:6)
    B. Name was John (John 1:6)
    C. Purpose (John 1:7)
       1. Bear witness of the light (John 1:8)
       2. That all may believe through Him (John 1:7)
    D. He was not the light

IV.   True light (John 1:9-10)
    A. Enlightens every man (John 1:9)
    B. Was in the world (John 1:10)
    C. World was made through Him (John 1:10)
    D. World did not know Him (John 1:10)

ADDITIONAL BIBLE STUDY STEPS

OUTLINE
John 3:1-12
Student Sample

I. Religious leader seeks verification of his opinions (1, 2).
   A. We know you come from God as a teacher (2b).
   B. The works you do prove your sanction by God (2c).

II. Jesus shows the true level of spiritual understanding of Nicodemus through dialogue on the rebirth (3-12).
   A. Jesus states that a man must be born again (3-8).
      1. Without spiritual birth, one cannot know or be acquainted with spiritual things (3).
         a. The flesh understands things of the flesh (6a).
         b. The spirit is *the* unique life that understands things of the Spirit (6b).
      2. Without spiritual birth, one cannot enter the kingdom of God (5).
         a. The flesh reaps rewards of the flesh (6a).
         b. The spirit reaps rewards of the spirit (6b).
      3. Do not be surprised at this statement, for that is of the flesh (7, 8).
         a. Your ignorance of the wind you experience doesn't cause you to marvel (8a).
            1) You don't know where it comes from (8b).
            2) You don't know where it goes (8c).
         b. People born of the Spirit sense spiritual things, although they don't understand them perfectly (8d).
   B. Nicodemus stubbornly relies on human understanding (4, 9).
      1. How can a birth happen to an old man? (4a)
      2. How would it be possible for me to enter my mother's womb and be born a second time? (4b)
      3. What you're saying isn't making any sense. (9)
   C. Jesus claims the disciples and Himself have experienced the second birth (11)
   D. Jesus asks, "How can you call yourself a religious leader?" (10, 11)
      1. You say you don't understand this?
      2. You refuse the evidence you yourself stated when you came in here.
   E. "Why do you all bother asking me questions about heaven when you can't grasp the basics of what must happen to you right here?" (12)

OUTLINE

Galatians 5:2-12

Student Sample

I. The General Principles (2-6)
  A. Reasons for not living under law (2-4)
    1. Results of receiving circumcision (2, 3)
      a. Christ of no benefit (2)
      b. under obligation to keep the whole law (3)
    2. Results of seeking to be justified by the law (4)
      a. severed from Christ (4a)
      b. fallen from grace (4b)
  B. Reasons for living under grace (5, 6)
    1. Because of source of ultimate righteousness (5)
      a. through the Spirit (5)
      b. by faith (5)
    2. Because of the results of being in Christ (6)
      a. circumcision or uncircumcision meaningless (6a)
      b. faith through love all important (6b)
II. The Specific Situation (7-12)
  A. The change in the Galatians (7-9)
    1. Question concerning the change (7)
      a. past performance remembered (7a)
      b. cause for present hindrance asked (7b)
    2. Evaluation concerning the change (8, 9)
      a. present persuasion not of God (8)
      b. pertinent illustration (9)
  B. The people involved in the controversial change (10-12)
    1. Paul's future expectations (10)
      a. Paul's expression of confidence in the Galatians (10a)
      b. Paul's warning of judgment on the disturbers (10b)
    2. The impossibility of Paul's preaching circumcision (11)
      a. Paul would be persecuted (11a)
      b. the offense of the cross would be removed (11b)
    3. Paul's desire concerning those troubling the Galatians (12)

ADDITIONAL BIBLE STUDY STEPS

OUTLINE

Ephesians 4:11-16
Student Sample

I. Repertoire of spiritual gifts (11)
    A. Apostles (11a)
    B. Prophets (11b)
    C. Evangelists (11c)
    D. Pastors (11d)
    E. Teachers (11e)

II. Reason for spiritual gifts (12)
    A. For the equipping of the saints for the work of service
        to the building up of the body of Christ

III. Time of spiritual gifts (13)
    A. Until we attain the unity of the faith (13a)
    B. Until we attain the knowledge of the Son of God (13b)
        1. To maturity
        2. To Christ's stature

IV. Result of spiritual gifts (14-16)
    A. No longer children (14)
        1. Tossed here and there (14a)
        2. Carried about by every wind of doctrine (14b)
        3. Carried about by the trickery of men (14c)
        4. Carried about by craftiness in deceitful scheming
            (14d)
    B. We are to grow in all aspects into Christ (15, 16)
        1. Properly fitted together in the body (15, 16a)
        2. Properly held together by each joint (16b)
        3. Each part individually working (16c)
            a. causing growth of body
            b. building body in love

• **PARAPHRASE**

Another helpful step in understanding and teaching the Scriptures is doing a paraphrase to see the details of the passage you are studying.

A. How to paraphrase: to paraphrase a passage of Scripture is to study a passage and to restate it in your own words.

B. How a paraphrase can help you:
1. To paraphrase a passage requires that you think through each thought and word of the passage sufficiently enough to restate it. It will clarify your thinking on the truths presented.
2. It also can help your communication of those spiritual truths to others. You should seek to express the truths in terms that would be understood easily by someone else today. Put it into contemporary English. (*J. B. Phillip's New Testament* and Kenneth Taylor's *Living Gospels, Living Letters,* and *Living Prophecies* are modern paraphrases that would be good to study as examples.)

C. How to use variety in paraphrase:
1. A normal paraphrase: One type of paraphrase would be to take the passage one phrase at a time and rephrase it in your own words. It is important not to change just a few words in the passage but to change the entire phrase and leave almost no word the same.
2. A condensed paraphrase: You might try to boil a passage down to perhaps two-thirds, one-half or even one-third its original length. Try not to omit the essential parts. This type is especially good for long passages or for narrative passages.
3. An expanded paraphrase: You might expand the passage perhaps even to as much as twice its original length. You would be seeking to explain fully the meaning of the passage. It would include interpretations and explanations of things that were not clear. This would be very appropriate for doctrinal passages rather than narrative.

4. Use of imagination: Use your imagination in paraphrasing.
   a. Sometimes try changing illustrations into modern illustrations. Instead of saying the Word of God is "sharper than any two-edged sword," you might say it is "sharper than any surgeon's scalpel."
   b. You might imagine that you are writing to some particular person today. For example, you want to paraphrase one of Paul's epistles. So, you imagine that you are writing a friend who is a new Christian, and you try to explain the truths found in the epistle to him in the language that you might normally use if you were writing him a letter.

• THE TOPICAL STUDY

I. What is a topical study?

   A. Instead of studying a book or a portion of a book, in a topical study you are seeking to determine what is taught by Scripture on a particular subject. For example, you may wish to study what the Bible has to say about the subject "laziness."
   B. For a doctrinal study, you simply choose a doctrinal topic, such as the doctrine of justification.
   C. Because of time available, you may choose to limit your subject by limiting the portion of Scripture from which you obtain your material. For example: "The doctrine of Christ in Colossians," or "The use of the term *children* in the writings of John."
   D. The key to a good topical study is the selection of a good topic.

II. How to locate material for a topical study.

   A. Use a concordance. Look up the use of words which relate to your topic.

B. Cross-references. Once you have found some passages that relate to your topic, you can often find cross-references from these to other passages.

C. Bible dictionary. This may give you both good information and further scriptural references concerning your topic.

D. Subject listings. Sometimes reference Bibles list Scripture references according to subject. There are also topical Bibles, such as *Nave's Topical Bible*, which write out the entire text of various passages that relate to certain topics.

E. If you have limited your subject to a certain portion of Scripture, such as "St. Paul's prayers in his epistles," you might have to read or scan the material to locate the sections you want.

III. How to arrange the material you locate.

A. Once you have located your material, study it and make any notes concerning things that you want to remember.

B. Study your notes and categorize them. Group together similar ideas under similar topics. The different emphasis of the various verses will suggest various topics for the outline. As you begin to categorize verses, this may suggest to your mind further study in certain areas of the topic.

C. Next work your material into a logical outline. Begin with a rough tentative outline and polish it as you progress. Try to fit all of your material into the outline.

IV. How to make applications from a topical study.
See principles of application on pages 98 and 99.

ADDITIONAL BIBLE STUDY STEPS

● THE BIOGRAPHICAL STUDY

(This is really a specialized topical study — the topic here being a person.)

I. How to research a biographical study.

    A. Things to keep in mind.
        1. You will find your material in a similar manner as you would for a topical study.
        2. Be careful if you use a Bible dictionary that you do not let it do your thinking for you or predispose your mind to certain conclusions. It may be best to read the Bible dictionary article *after* you have done your own thinking.
        3. Some Bible characters have more than one name, such as Saul for Paul, Cephas and Simon for Peter, Israel for Jacob. Be sure you have all the references for the person.
        4. Sometimes biblical names are used for more than one person. Saul, John, Mary, etc. Be sure that you are reading the person you want to study.
        5. Some characters have such a large portion of Scripture devoted to them that you may want to limit your study to a particular phase of that person's life. (Example: The prayer life of the apostle Paul.)

    B. Things to look for. The following suggests certain items to look for in doing a research. Sometimes, because of lack of information available on an individual, it will not be possible to find all of these things. This does not pretend to be an exhaustive list but simply a guide. You will think of other areas for study as you find information on the person being studied.
        1. Background
            a. What were the circumstances surrounding his birth — when, where, etc.?
            b. Who were his parents and family? What were they like? What was their spiritual condition?

    c. How did environment and early training influence his later life?

    d. What other factors prepared him for later life?

2. Major factors of adult life.

    a. What were his major occupation and achievements in life?

    b. What was he most noted for?

    c. What people were important in his life? His friends, his enemies, his family? What influence did others have on him and vice versa?

    d. Geography—where did he live and minister?

    e. What was his relationship to God? How did this affect his life and accomplishments?

    f. Did he write any portion of Scripture? What does it show about him?

3. Major events.

    a. What were the major events of his life? What were the major crises?

    b. What were the various periods or phases of his life? What were the pivotal points which divide these periods?

    c. What was the manner, cause and effect of his death?

4. Character.

    a. What sort of character did he have?

    b. What were his strong points?

    c. What were his weak points?

    d. What were the causes and results of the strong and weak points of his character?

    e. What were his specific faults and sins? What were the consequences of this?

    f. What was his general attitude toward life and toward others?

    g. What was his spiritual status?

    h. What basic principles seemed to guide his life and his work?

ADDITIONAL BIBLE STUDY STEPS

    5. Influence.
- a. What effect did he have on his contemporaries?
- b. What influence did he have on subsequent history?
- c. Concerning an Old Testament character, find out the following:
  - 1) Could he be considered a type of Christ? If so, in what way?
  - 2) How does the New Testament represent him, if it does?

    6. Details. Do not overlook details. They add color and often prove to be very significant.

II. How to organize your material in a biographical study.

- A. You may want to arrange your material in outline form. Follow the directions on outlining (see pp. 123-126). Some of the above suggestions (B under I.) of what to look for may suggest other categories.
- B. You may want to write a character sketch of the person.
- C. Conclude your story by writing a section on suggested personal applications to your own life. These could be learned either from the positive or negative side of the life studied.

Samples

BOOK CHART

John 1-21

Student Sample

Chapters	1	2	3	4	5	6	7	8	9	10
Chapter Titles	Word Becomes Flesh	Water to Wine	Born Again	Living Water & Off. Son Healed	Pool Healing	Bread of Life	Proc. Cause Trouble	Light of World (Jesus)	Blind Man Healed	Jesus Good Shepherd
Paragraph Titles	:1-5 Word is Light	:1-11 Water to wine	:1-15 Nic. & man's rebirth	:1-6 Sam. woman	:1-9 Man healed at pool	:1-14 Mult. fed	:1-9 Disciples feast at table	:1-11 Jesus & adultss.	:1-12 Jesus heals blind man	:1-6 Enter by Christ
	:6-8 Witness to come	:12 To Capernaum	:16-21 Truth or consequence	:7-15 Living water	:10-18 Sab. control	:15 Jesus withdraws	:10-13 Jesus talks of feast	:12-20 Jesus gives witness	:13-17 Blind man quest. by Phar.	:7-18 Christ is door
	:9-13 Jesus Light	:13-22 Temple cleansed	:22-24 To Judea to baptize	:16-26 Truth revealed to woman	:19-29 Son judges	:16-21 Water walk	:14,24 Sud. proc in temple	:21-30 Warn. unbelief	:18-23 Phar. quest. parents	:19-21 Jews look at Jesus as demon
	:14-18 Jesus made flesh	:23-25 Jesus knows man	:25-30 John steps down	:27-30 Village revival	:30-41 W'k of Son	:22-24 Search for Jesus	:25-31 Attempt arrest	:31-38 Jews defend race	:24-34	:22-30 Jesus' Word is proof
	:19-23 John the Baptist		:31-36 Spirit without measure	:31-38 Harvest ripe		:25-38 Sermon on life bread	:32-36 Jesus puzzles crowd	:39-47 Jews don't hear Jesus	:35-41 Jesus talks with blind man	:31-39 Jesus' belief by Jesus' works
	:24-28			:39-42 Sam. believe		:34-40 Son giver of life	:37-39 Last day proc.	:48-59 Jesus almost stoned		:40-42 many believed in Jordan
	:29-34 Dove comes			:43-45 Jesus not rec'd		:41-51 Discourse to murmurers	:40-44 Doubt. Jesus			
	:35-42 1st two disciples			:46-54 Off. son healed		:52-59 Life blood	:45-53			
	:43-51 Phil. & Nath. fol. Jesus					:60-65 Quest disciples				
						:66-71 Peter's affirm.				

140

BOOK CHART
John (cont'd.)

11	12	13	14	15	16	17	18	19	20	21
Lazarus Raised	Triumphal Entry	Jesus Washes Feet of Disc.	Jesus: True Way of Life	Love One Another	Christ: Giver of Spirit Life	Christ's Prayers	Jesus Arrested	Uplifted Savior	Christ Conquers Death	Parting Words
:1-4 Jesus hears Laz. ill	:1-8 Mary anoints Jesus	:1-11 Jesus cleans feet	:1-7 Jesus prepares place	:1-11 Jesus true vine	:1-4 Beware of world	:1-5 Prayer glorific.	:1-11 Jesus arrest. & betrayal	:1-2 Christ crowned	:1-15 Resurrection	:1-14 Christ appears to 7 disciples at Sea of Galilee
:5-16 Jesus goes to Lazarus	:9-11 Jews visit & plan to kill Jesus	:12-20 Servant less than master	:8-11 Phil. asked to see Father	:12-17 Jesus com. disciples love one another	:5-11 Coming of Spirit	:6-19 Disciple's prayer	:12-14 Jesus taken to auth.	:13-18 Jesus turned over to mob	:16-18 Jesus reveals Himself to Mary	:15-25 Jesus foretells Peter's death
:17-27 Martha believes	:12-19 Triumphal entry	:21-30 Judas leaves	:12-14 Greater works promised	:18-27 Hated of world	:12-15 Nature of Spirit	:20-25 Church prayer	:15-18 Peter's 1st denial	:19-22 Pilate makes sign for cross	:19-23 Christ 1st app. to disciples	
:28-37 Jesus wept	:20-26 Lose life or live?	:31-35 Love one another	:15-17 Jesus promises Spirit		:16-24 Jesus' farewell		:19-24 1st quest & struck	:23-25 Gambling for Christ's garment	:24-25 Thomas sees to believe	
:38-44 Lazarus raised	:27-36 God glorifies Jesus' name	:36-38 Peter's denial foretold	:18-24 Homeward bound		:25-28 Christ's origin		:25-27 2nd & 3rd denial	:26-27 Motherly love	:26-29 Thomas believes	
:45-53 Priest prophesied death	:37-43 Reason for man's disbelief		:25-31 Peace is promised		:29-33 Christ overcomes world		:28-32 Jesus taken to Pilate	:28-32 Christ's death	:30-31 Purpose of Word	
:54-57 Jesus wanted at Passover	:44-50 Sum. Jesus' claims						:33-38 Pilate asks truth?	:31-37 Proph. fulfilled		
							:39-40 Barabbas released	:31-42 Jesus entombed		

141

Chapters	1	2	3	4	5	6	7	8	9	10
Chapter Titles	Jesus Proclaimed	Water to Wine/Temp Scourge	Nic.-New Birth! John's Test.	Woman at Well/Liv- ing Water	Sab & Pall. Controv. Jdgmt./Wit	Bread of Life feeds 5,000	World Hates (Jesus Say) Come to Me	The Truth Will Set You Free	Blind Man Healed Fights Ldrs	Jesus as Shepherd
Paragraph Titles	:1-5 Jesus proclaimed as the Word :6-8 Jesus proclaimed through Jn :9-13 Jesus proclmed to us :14-18 Jesus pro- clmed as God manf'd :19-28 Jesus proclmed by John's wit. :29-34 Jesus pro- clmed as Lamb of God :35-42 Jesus proclmed by Andrew [Messiah, Rabbi] :43-51 Jesus proclmed by Nath.	:1-11 Jesus turns water to wine at wedding (1st sign) :12 Jesus, His family, disciples go to Cap- ernaum :13-22 Jesus throws dealers out of temple :23-25 Many in Jerusalem believe [but He knows]	:1-15 Jesus tells Nic. God is spirit'l birth :16-21 God loves world and sent Son :22-30 Jesus- increase John- decrease :31-36 John's testimony (Believe! Obey)	:1-26 Sam. woman liv'g wat'r God is Spirit :27-38 Jesus' food: will of Father :39-42 Many Sam. believe :43-45 Galileans receive Jesus :46-54 2nd sign- nobleman's son healed	:1-9 Pallet & poolside Jesus per- sec'd; break'g Sabbath :19-29 Pw'r given Son-jdgmt :30-47 5-phase wit'ns of the Son	:1-14 Bread for 5,000 :15 With- drew to mt.; crowd would crown Him king :16-21 Jesus walks on water :22-41 Jesus; brd of life :42-52 Jesus lvg bread fr. heaven :53-59 Eat His flsh drk His bld gain life :60-65 Jesus' wds Sp. & lfe :66-71 Peter's testimony	:1-9 Wld hates Jesus :10-13 Jesus at- tends feast secretly :14-24 Jesus' learned teaching :25-36 Jesus' appeal to unbeliev'g :37-44 Crowd divides :45-53 Off. puzl'd Pharisees firm	:1-11 Who'll stone adulteress :12-20 Phar. de- mand & rec. tes- timonies :21-30 All things please Father :31-47 Father controv. who con- victs Me of sin? :48-59 Father glorifies Me	:1-12 Blind man (whose sin) healed :13-23 Phar. quest. him & parents :24-34 Quest. again, casts out synagogue :35-41 Jesus looks up outcast: believes	:1-7 The sheep fol- low shepherd :8-18 Jesus as the good shepherd :19-21 Jews di- vide :22-30 Who are You? [I & F. one] :31-39 Rebuke-I am Son of God :40-42 beyond Jordan many be- lieve
Key Verse: Key Word:	1 The Word	11, 23-25 1st mircl; believe	5-7, 16 love, birth	14 liv'g wtr	24, 36 jdgmt, witnesses	35,63 bread	7, 37-38 come	32 free truth	5 retaliation	8, 11, 14 sheep

11	12	13	14	15	16	17	18	19	20	21
Jesus Raises Laz. From Dead	Final Hrs Pub. Min.	Slave/Mstr New Comm'd	Farewell Discourse to Disciples	Greater Love Has No Man	The Joy of Believers	Final Prayer	Jesus Is Taken	Death of Jesus	The Risen Christ	Last Appearance & Commands
:1-16 Laz. dies :17-29 Jesus: resurrection & life :30-37 Jesus weeps :38-44 Laz. "Come forth" :45-46 More believe :47-53 Jesus' death plotted :54-57 Jesus seeks refuge (in Ephraim)	:1-8 Mary anoints Jesus (poor always) :9-11 Many come, see Jesus & Laz. :12-19 Palm leaves & triumph. Eyes blind hearts are hardened :20-26 Hour & the seed (dies to give life) :27-36 :37-43 Jesus' last pub. discourse :44-50 Jesus sums up His claims	:1-11 Jesus washes disciples' feet :12-20 Slave not greater than mstr :21-30 Judas receives morsel fr. Jesus :31-35 New comd'mt (love one another) :36-38 Jesus predicts Peter's denial	:1-24 Jesus' farewell discourse & Holy Sp. promised :25-31 Sp.—new teacher	:1-27 Jesus the true vine—love one another	:1-24 The work of the Spirit :25-33 Jesus—I have overcome the world	:1-26 Jesus' farewell prayer	:1-11 The betrayal :12-14 Jesus taken :15-18 Peter's 1st denial :19-24 Jesus 1st questioning :25-27 Peter's 2nd & 3rd denials :28-32 Jesus delivered before Pilate :33-40 Jesus—My kingdom is not of this world	:1-16 Sentenced before Pilate :17-22 Jesus carries cross & is crucified :23-27 Soldiers gamble for Jesus' robe; "Behold your son" :28-30 Last wds :31-37 Confirm'n of death :38-42 Laid in tomb	:1-10 Visit tomb; discover miss'g bdy :11-18 Risen Christ talks to Mary :19-23 Appears to disciples :24-25 Doubting Thomas demands prf. :26-29 Thru closed door & Thomas convinced :30-31 Written that you may believe	:1-15 Jesus appears to disciples fishing :15-23 "3 quest's for Peter" "Follow Me" "Tend My sheep" :24 Author-eyewitness account :25 World would not contain books
:25-26 live if die	:24-25,35-36 triumphal entry	:34 new comm'd	:6 farewell	:13 vine	:33 overcome	:26 manifest glorify	:36 betrayal	:11,30 death	:31 risen	:17 tend

143

BOOK CHART

John 1-6

Student Sample

Chapters	1	2	3	4	5	6
Chapter Titles	*Jesus Recognized*	*Wedding Wine & Temple Cleansed*	*Born Again Through Believing in Christ*	*Samaritan Revival & A Nobleman's Son*	*The Sabbatical Pallet Contrv. Jdgmt.-Witns.*	*5000 Fed & Sea Calmed by Bread of Life*
Paragraph Titles	:1-5 Recognized as the Word :6-8 Recognized by *John* 9:13 Recognized by *us* :14-18 Recognized by His glory :19-28 Recognized by religious leaders :29-34 Recognized as *Lamb of God* :35-42 Recognized by *Andrew* :43-51 Recognized by *Nathaniel*	:1-11 Wedding in Cana :12 To Capernaum :13-22 Temple cleansing :23-25 Jesus knows men	:1-15 Born again :16-21 By believing :22-30 In Christ :31-36 Christ, witness from heaven	:1-27 Jesus witnesses to a woman :28-38 The harvest is white :39-42 Revival breaks loose :43-45 Prophet without honor :46 Nobleman's son healed	:1-9 Walking with the pallet :10-18 Jesus persecuted :19-29 All judgment to the Son :30-47 Witness of John, Father's words rejected through pride	:1-14 Feeding of 5,000 :15-21 Sea calmed :22-40 Bread of Life :41-51 Eat and live :52-59 The Jews grumble :60-65 The disciples puzzled :66-71 Judas will betray
KEY VERSE: KEY WORD:	:14 Tabernacle	:11 Sign	:3 Believe	:39 Testimony	:24 Life	:35 Bread

144

BOOK CHART

Ephesians

Student Sample

Chapters	1	2	3	4	5	6
Chapter Titles	New Position in Christ	New Life in Christ	New Love in Christ	New Unity in Christ	New Walk in Christ	New Armor in Christ
Paragraph Titles	:1-2 Hello :3-14 Our inheritance :15-23 Paul's prayer for us	:1-10 Made alive in Christ :11-22 Gentile and Jew together in Christ	:1-13 God's secret revealed :14-19 God's love personified :20-21 God's generosity revealed	:1-16 The equipping of the body :17-24 The walking of the body :25-32 The holiness of the body	:1-2 Walk in love :3-14 Walk in purity :15-21 Walk in the Spirit :22-33 Walk in oneness	:1-4 Family :5-9 Slaves and masters :10-20 Armor of God :21-24 Closing remarks
Key Verse: Key Word:	9 Promise	5 Made alive	6 Follow heirs	15,16 Whole body	18 Walk	11 Armor

145

BOOK CHART
Galatians
Student Sample

Chapters	1	2	3	4	5	6
Chapter Titles	Paul's Autobiography of Early Life	Gospel of Grace to the Gentiles	Law vs. Grace	Freedom in Christ	Walk Free in the Spirit	Exhortations
Paragraph Titles	:1-5 Greeting :6-10 One true gospel to preach :11-17 Paul's commission to preach :18-24 Paul's reputation in Jerusalem	:1-10 Approval of apostles :11-12 Paul confronts Peter	:1-14 Laws not the way :15-22 Jesus and the law :23-29 Oneness in Christ	:1-7 Rights of sonship in Christ :8-11 Freemen returning to slavery :12-20 Paul's disappointment :21-31 Illustration of Isaac & Ishmael	:1 Stay free :2-12 Legalism excluded :13-15 Love is the outcome of freedom :16-24 Walk in the Spirit :25-26 Humility in the Spirit	:1-5 Bear one another's burdens :6-10 Reaping in the Spirit :11-16 Boast only in the cross :17-18 Summary testimony and closing
Key Verse: Key Word:	12 Revelation	2 Gentiles	13 Law	31 Free	22 Spirit	10 Reap

Sample
BOOK CHART
with Chapter and Paragraph Titles of
Galatians

Chapters	1	2	3	4	5	6
Chapter Titles	*Paul's Unperverted Gospel*	*Paul's Apostolic Authority*	*Justification by Faith, Not Law*	*Freedom by Sonship Not Slavery*	*Freedom by the Spirit, Not the Flesh*	*Practical Outworking of Grace*
Paragraph Titles	:1-5 Salutation :6-10 Different gospel :11-17 Revealed gospel :18-24 Paul's early contacts with other apostles	:1-10 Recognition of Paul's apostleship :11-21 Paul's confrontation with Peter	:1-14 Law vs. faith :15-22 The character of the law :23-24 The law was tutor	:1-7 Slavery to sonship :8-11 Warning not to return to slavery :12-20 Concern for fickle Galatians :21-31 O.T. allegory on freedom	:1 Exhorted to stand :2-12 Obligation to law under circumstances :13-15 Fulfillment of the law through love :16-24 The flesh vs. the Spirit :25-26 Exhorted to walk by the Spirit	:1-5 Proper attitude for others & self :6-10 Sowing & reaping :11-16 :17 Plea to end trouble :18 Benediction

Sample
BOOK CHART
with Chapter Titles only
Romans 1-8

Ch. 1 Heathen Without Excuse	Ch. 2 Moral & Relig. Man W/out Excuse	Ch. 3 World W/o. Exc. Just. by Faith	Ch. 4 Just. by Faith O.T. Message	Ch. 5 Blessings of J. by Faith & Two Spheres of Existence	Ch. 6 Identified w/ Christ	Ch. 7 Law School	Ch. 8 Christ in Me

SAMPLE

Scripture	Observations		Interpretive Questions
"In the beginning was the Word, and the Word was with God, and the Word was God. He was in the beginning with God. All things came into being through Him; and apart from Him nothing came into being that has come into being. In Him was life; and the life was the light of men. And the light shines in the darkness; and the darkness did not comprehend it."	WHO:	The Word, God, He, the light, the life, Him, men	Who is the Word? Is it Jesus? Who is the Life? Who does "the men" refer to? (All men, certain men, etc.)
	WHAT:	John is describing: The Word was in the beginning The Word was with God The Word was God He was in the beginning All things came into being through Him In Him (Jesus) is the light – shines on men Darkness doesn't overpower the light The life was the light of men	What does "Word" mean? What does "darkness" refer to? What does it mean "the life was the light of men"? What kind of "life" does this mean? (eternal, abundant, etc.)
	WHEN:	Creation or the creating process has already taken place... "nothing came into being that has"	When was "the life" the light of men? (always, period of time)
	WHERE:	In the beginning was the Word The Word was with God He was in the beginning with God	
	WHY:		Why does John call Jesus the "Word"? Why does John contain John 1:1-5 in his gospel account? (heresy, etc.) Why does it say "the darkness did not overcome it" (Is the battle over with)?
	HOW:	Creation came about by an infinite, eternal God creating.	How does the "light" shine? (through creation, men, etc.)

OBSERVATION CHART

John 1:1-5 (cont'd)

Scripture	Observations	Interpretive Questions
	ALIKE: God and Word are alike In the beginning: Creation happens (much like Genesis 1:1] Jesus' life: the light of men (:1] In the beginning was the Word and (:2] He was in the beginning with God. All things created by Him: Nothing came into being except through Him. Word being in the beginning; Word was God; Word is Creator **DIFFERENT:** Darkness and light Light shining and darkness not overpower **REPEATED:** The verb *was*; the noun *Word* the *Word was* in the beginning the *Word was* with God the *Word was* God He *was* in the beginning with God In Him *was* life the life *was* the light of men the phrase: "In the beginning" *was* the Word He *was in the beginning* with God the verb: *came* All things *came* . . . apart from Him nothing *came*	

150

OBSERVATION CHART

John 1:1-5 (cont'd)

Scripture	Observations	Interpretive Questions
	the noun: the life	
	In Him was life . . . the life was	
	the noun: Him	
	In Him; through Him; from Him	
	the noun: darkness; shines in the darkness, etc.	
	the noun: the life	
	CAUSE AND EFFECT:	
	cause effect	
	Jesus being the life; the light of men	
	cause effect	
	All things came into being nothing else came	
	into being	
	cause effect	
	Jesus being from the He was with God	
	beginning He was God	
	He was creator	
	cause effect	
	the darkness cannot	
	The light shines overcome	
	GENERAL TO SPECIFIC:	
	From Jesus being in the beginning—with God;	
	finally being God	
	From Jesus being source of creation—	
	finally Jesus being only source	

151

OBSERVATION CHART

John 1:1-5 (cont'd)

Scripture	Observations	Interpretive Questions
	From Jesus being the life to finally being the light of men CONNECTIVES: In; and; with; into; from; that; of PROMISES: The darkness did not overpower it.	

SAMPLE

OBSERVATION CHART

2 Timothy 3:16-17

Student Sample

Scripture	Observations	Interpretive Questions
2 Timothy 3:16 "All Scripture is inspired by God and profitable	All of the Scriptures are included "Is" – currently – not becoming – verb of being. God is the source – not man – even not by the writers 1) "and" – equally important that inspired and profitable 2) has been inspired for my benefit 3) all profitable – not just some	What does "inspired" mean? How is it profitable? – explained in the verse. What does profitable mean?
for teaching	The way is profitable – things profitable for. I can use it to teach me and others. It will tell me what I should know	What does it teach me?
for reproof for correction for training in righteousness"	It will show me where I am wrong It will show me what I should do It will show me how to do what I should It gives help for right from wrong living	What does reproof mean? Correction from what? – wrong in God's sight. Training in what? and for what? What or whose righteousness? What does righteousness mean?
2 Timothy 3:17 "that	Purpose clause (dependent) Can't have result without the cause!	
the man of God may be adequate (thoroughly) equipped	The above is for the man who wants to be God's man – not his own control I can be totally ready for everything that may come my way.	What does "man of God" imply? What does "adequate" mean and include? What kind of equipment will I receive?
for every good work"	I will have all the resources I will need to fulfill any and all good works God will ever call me to do. (Philippians 4:13, 1 Thessalonians 5:24)	What is a good work?

153

OBSERVATION CHART

Acts 1:1-8

Student Sample

Scripture		Observations	Interpretive Questions
:1	1. WHO:	Luke (author), Theophilus, Jesus	1. Why the people of Theophilus?
	2. WHAT:	treatise (book of Acts)	2. Why called treatise?
	3. WHERE:	Theophilus – was a person, not a place	
	4. WHY:	Telling of all Jesus began to do and preach	
:2	1. WHO:	Christ, Holy Ghost, apostles	1. How does the Holy Spirit give His commandments?
	2. WHEN:	The day He was taken up	
	3. WHY:	Give commandments to apostles through Holy Spirit	2. What is ministry of Holy Spirit?
	4. HOW:	Ministry of the Holy Spirit	
:3	1. WHO:	Jesus, them (people), God	1. How did He show infallible proofs?
	2. WHAT:	Showing infallible proofs, speaking of things of kingdom	2. How did He need to show Himself alive?
	3. WHEN:	After his passion, during 40 days	3. What was the passion?
	4. WHY:	To show Himself alive	
	5. HOW:	Proofs, speakings	
:4	1. WHO:	Jesus, them (people), Father	1. Why were they assembled?
	2. WHAT:	Commandments to them	2. What was the Father's promise?
	3. WHEN:	When assembled, when waiting for Father	
	4. WHERE:	Not depart from Jerusalem	
	5. WHY:	Wait for promise	
	6. HOW:	By the Holy Spirit	
:5	1. WHO:	John, ye (people), Holy Ghost, Christ (speaking)	1. What is difference of baptism of Holy Spirit and of water?
	2. WHAT:	Baptism of Holy Spirit	

154

OBSERVATION CHART

Acts 1:1-8 (cont'd)

Scripture		Observations	Interpretive Questions
:6	3. WHEN:	Not many days hence	
	4. HOW:	By Holy Ghost	
	1. WHO:	They (people), Christ	1. Was the questioning before or after the ascension?
	2. WHAT:	Questioning of Him	2. What did He mean by His statement?
	3. WHEN:	The ascension	
	4. WHY:	About restoration of Israel	
	5. HOW:	Wonderment of what He meant	
:7	1. WHO:	Christ, people, Father	1. Why won't the Father let them know when times?
	2. WHAT:	Explanation of God's works	
	3. WHEN:	Not know times or seasons	
	4. WHY:	Because the Father hasn't given to them when	
	5. HOW:	By the Father's own power	
:8	1. WHO:	Christ (speaking), ye (people), Holy Ghost, witnesses, people of Jerusalem, Samaria, Judea, and all the earth	1. How do they receive Holy Spirit?
			2. Why is it after Christ's ascension?
	2. WHAT:	Power after receiving Holy Spirit	
	3. WHEN:	After Holy Spirit is come upon them	
	4. WHERE:	In Jerusalem, Samaria, Judea and all the earth	
	5. WHY:	To witness of Christ	
	6. HOW:	By receiving power of Holy Spirit	

155

OBSERVATION CHART

John 3:1-8
Student Sample

Scripture	Observations	Interpretive Questions
"Now there was a man of the Pharisees, named Nicodemus, a ruler of the Jews; this man came to Him by night, and said to Him, "Rabbi, we know that You have come from God as a teacher; for no one can do these signs that You do unless God is with him." Jesus answered and said to him, "Truly, truly, I say to you, unless one is born again, he cannot see the kingdom of God." John 3:1-3	Reappears in John 7:50; 19:39; Ex. 12:12-26; Ps. 19:9 Jesus was in Jerusalem at the time of the Passover. Nicodemus (Nic.) had evidently heard of or seen Jesus earlier and had sought to find Him. A number of reasons seem to exist as to why he might have come at night: 1. His duties as a ruler, teacher and Pharisee might have prevented him from coming or seeking Him during the day. 2. As a man with a probable in-depth knowledge of the O.T., he probably was looking for the Messiah also, as were many of the Jews, and hearing of Jesus' miracles was seeking to find out if Jesus were the Christ, but was afraid of what others Jews – especially other Pharisees – might say if they saw him speaking with Jesus. 3. He might have felt that it would be less crowded at night and thus he would have a better opportunity of speaking at length to Jesus. Evidence that Nic. might have felt that Jesus was the Messiah:	John 3:1 What was a Jewish ruler? What was a Pharisee? Why did the desire to see Jesus? Was his life spiritually empty? Was there much difference in titles given to the rulers? John 3:2 Why did he go to see Jesus to begin with? Why did he go at night? Was he speaking on behalf of the Pharisees or was he with somebody? Do you think he was suspicious of Jesus in any way? Did he follow Jesus to see what he had done (signs)? Do you think he had a lot of respect for Jesus? John 3:3 Did Jesus more or less command Nic. to be reborn? Was Jesus saying much about Himself, concerning Spirit?

156

OBSERVATION CHART

John 3:1-8 (cont'd)

Scripture	Observations	Interpretive Questions
	1. Jesus had no sooner started His ministry than Nic. was already seeking him. 2. Calls Jesus a Rabbi, meaning that he *knew* Jesus was a teacher. 3. Says *we know that you have come from* God (no small statement. Nic. would not have said that, being a Pharisee, unless he had reason to believe that Jesus were come from God.) However, he realizes that Jesus is not ordinary teacher by adding "from God." Nic. recognizes the miracles of Jesus as not mere good, fancy, tricks or catchy illusion, or works of Satan, but as good works, unto the glory of God. He also sees them as a sign; things the Jews were to look for in the coming Messiah. In saying "no one" he makes light mention of the fact that there haven't been too many people around pulling off signs or miracles of this particular nature. The Greek work for signs used in this context can also be translated "miracle." Nic. again deserves a hand, for here, he is giving Jesus credit for performing the miracles, or at least recognizing that He is being used by God. He also states that the "we" making the statement believe to to the point of knowing that God is with Jesus.	Is this spiritual re-birth required in order to get to heaven? kingdom of God? Is there a difference between the kingdom of God and kingdom of heaven?

OBSERVATION CHART

John 3:1-8 (cont'd)

Scripture	Observations	Interpretive Questions
	It seems possible, as evidenced by the phrasing, and bluntness of Nic.'s statement, that he was leading into questions that were really bugging him, like, "OK Jesus, I realize that you have God with You and You perform miracles or signs, but what I'd really like to know is, are You the Messiah?"	
	We learn in John 2:25 that Jesus knew all men and He knew what was in man.	
	It may also be observed that TRULY is simply a shortening of the word TRUTHFULLY—[you'd better listen twice].	
	YOU, ONE—progression Until now, the conversation between Nic. & Jesus has been seemingly superficial. Jesus goes from "you, Nic.," to a general; but never "one." The word "one" is very general. So general as to include all of humanity, and yet, so specific as to mean each individual, thus, so demonstrating that *each* individual of *all* of humanity must experience a new birth. So now Jesus is not just talking to Nic. but to all of man and involving each individual of humanity into the necessity of spiritual birth.	
	WE In the English use of the word "we," Nic. could be saying it as sort of a catch-all term to get himself out	

OBSERVATION CHART

John 3:1-8 (cont'd)

Scripture	Observations	Interpretive Questions
	of the picture and thus having a fictional third party recognize Jesus as a teacher come from God, possibly because:	

Observations (continued):

of the picture and thus having a fictional third party recognize Jesus as a teacher come from God, possibly because:

1. He was a Pharisee and didn't want to be making such statement on his own.
2. He was uncertain of who Jesus really was and thus, if Jesus were not the Christ, he could pass off his statement of "we" as meaning "they," but if Jesus were the Christ, he could be including himself in the pronoun "we." I could attribute such a cop-out to pride.

On the other hand, he could be sincere with his usage of "we" and could be including himself among a group of others who believe Jesus to be a teacher from God.

Possibilities of what group he might be representing or be a part of:

1. He could be representing a group of *Pharisees*, but it seems doubtful when we read John 7:48, however in Acts 23:8 we see that many of the Pharisees later believed in the resurrection;
2. He could be representing a group of the *rulers*, which seems more probable in the light of John 12:42;
3. He could be representing just a group of his *close friends*;
4. students;

OBSERVATION CHART

John 3:1-8 (cont'd)

Scripture	Observations	Interpretive Questions
	5. He could be using "we" as saying "the general concensus of opinion (of Jesus) of the people who have seen you is that you are a man come from God."	
	KNOW The K.J.V., R.S.V., N.E.B., N.A.S.B. all translate the Greek word whatever it is to "know," Philips translates as "realize." Either way, it carries with it an affirmation or admittance of what was believed to be true by "we."	
	Here is the clincher. Now Nic., or "we" make the commitment of recognition of Jesus as having come from God — Nic. is careful to put in "as a teacher."	
	Jesus and Nicodemus One must be born of water and Spirit to enter into heaven. Jesus assures him. A reply to Nicodemus' question concerning "if he was old." Man should be baptized in/by water. Man should be baptized by the Holy Spirit. The Spirit will indwell a new man. Key word: Born	*John 3:4* Was Nicodemus discouraged? Was he concerned about getting to heaven? Could he, an old man, be re-born? Was Nicodemus confused? Why was he so intently curious? Whatever happened to Nicodemus, was he reborn?

	Jesus continues with Nicodemus.
	Flesh gives birth to flesh and the Holy Spirit gives birth to spirit.
	Man connected with spirit and flesh.
	God provides the Spirit to dwell in man.
	Man can reproduce physically only.
	God provides the spiritual part.
	     Key word: Born
		John 3:5
		What does it mean to be born of water?
		   Do it as a cleansing of sin?
		What is it to be born of the Spirit?
		Is there any other way to get to heaven?
		Was Nicodemus too old?

"Nicodemus said to Him, 'How can a man be born when he is old? He cannot enter a second time into his mother's womb and be born, can he?' Jesus answered, 'Truly, truly, I say to you, unless one is born of water and the Spirit, he cannot enter into the kingdom of God. That which is born of the flesh is flesh; and that which is born of the Spirit is spirit. Do not marvel that I said		

OBSERVATION CHART

John 3:1-8 (cont'd)

Scripture	Observations	Interpretive Questions
to you, "You must be born again." The wind blows where it wishes and you hear the sound of it, but do not know where it comes from and where it is going; so is every one who is born of the Spirit." [John 3:4-8]	Jesus continues with Nicodemus. Says of all, you should/must have rebirth. Perhaps refers to all Pharisees, everybody. Don't be astonished because God is all-powerful – the Holy Spirit is powerful. Expect any miracle from God (almighty). Key word: Marvel The wind can be felt anywhere. It goes and comes and nobody can see it or tell where it's going next. The wind is not visible but you can feel it. You can see the results of the wind. You cannot see God, but you can see what He has done. You can't see the Spirit move into a person, but you can surely see the results! Praise God! Key word: Wind	Does man have to be baptized in church with water? Can he be baptized there with the Spirit? How long does the Spirit indwell (last)? *John 3:6* How does Jesus use this term "flesh"? Does man have any power other than physical? Does the Holy Spirit do all that is necessary in that baptism? When can this be done? Does man get more "power" after he has been baptized with the Spirit? *John 3:7* Do you feel this new birth? What was Nicodemus' reaction? Why did Jesus use "you"? Was there more than Nicodemus present? Did the Pharisees send Nicodemus to investigate Jesus (by asking from Nicodemus and the way Jesus answered him)?

161

OBSERVATION CHART

John 3:1-18 (cont'd)

Scripture	Observations	Interpretive Questions
		John 3:8
		Is somebody born of the Spirit completely changed?
		Can the Spirit enter a person that does not have much faith?
		Can it be predicted how somebody will act after being re-born?
		Can you see the results of the Spirit moving into a person?

SAMPLE

CROSS-REFERENCE CHART

Galatians 4:21-31
Student Sample

Verse	Cross-reference	Significance
v. 21	Luke 16:29	Both passages talk about men listening to what the law says.
v. 22	Genesis 16, 17, 18:1-21	These passages are the historical account of the births of Abraham's two sons, one (Ishmael) by a bond woman, Hagar, and one (Isaac) by the free woman, Sarah. The passages also show the conflict between the two women and between their sons. They also give God's promises in relation to the birth of Isaac.
v. 23	Romans 9:6-8	This shows that God sees a difference between children of promise and children of the flesh. The former are true children of God.
v. 24	1 Corinthians 10:11	The cross-reference states that the events that happened in the Old Testament were written for our instruction. Paul is using past events as an allegory of spiritual truth.
v. 25	(Bible dictionary)	Mount Sinai was the place where Moses received the Law.
v. 26	Revelation 21:2	The cross-reference tells of John's vision of the new Jerusalem coming down from heaven.
v. 27	Isaiah 54:1	This is the source of the quotation in verse 27. The content in Isaiah is one of rejoicing as a result of change from desolation to blessing.
v. 28	Galatians 3:29	The reference in both is that those in Christ are heirs according to praise.
v. 29	Galatians 5:11	Paul indicated that he is being persecuted because he is preaching according to the Spirit.
v. 30	Genesis 21:10, 12	This is the historical record of the casting out of Hagar and her son.
v. 31	Galatians 5:1	In verse 31, Paul draws the application of the allegory and this serves as a bridge to the exhortation that follows in 5:1.

KNOW YOUR BIBLE

INTERPRETATION OUTLINE

John 3:1 (KJV)
"Pharisees" (Sample No. 1)
Student Sample

I.   Old Testament relation to the Pharisees
   A. *Pharisee:* One of the three prominent societies of Judaism, and the most influential.
   B. *Circumcision:* The cutting off of the foreskin of a male, rite instituted by God as a sign of the covenant between Abraham and Him, to show Abraham's descendants they were God's own.
   C. *Law of Moses:* The summary of God's requirement of man in the Ten Commandments.
   D. *Jews:* God's chosen people — anyone of the Hebrew race returned from captivity.
   E. *Tribe of Benjamin:* Paul the Pharisee, descendant of. Tribe from one of the sons of Jacob.
   F. *Synagogue:* Jewish institution for the exposition of the Old Testament.
   G. *Rabbi:* Teacher of the Law.

II. New Testament relation to Pharisees
   A. *Scribes:* Class of learned men who made systematic study of the Law.
   B. *Jews:*
   C. *Paul:* Former Pharisee and persecutor of Jews, turned to be greatest apostle.
   D. *Publican:* Under-collector of Roman revenue; hated by Jews.
   E. *Fast:* Abstinence from food and drink.
   F. *Proselyte:* Foreign residents.
   G. *Phylacteries:* Leather boxes worn by Jewish males on forehead and left arm.
   H. *Damascus:* Ancient city of Syria, close to Paul's conversion.
   I. *Nicodemus:* Leading Pharisee and ruler of Jews converted to Christianity.

III. Characteristics of:
   A. Jewish sect . . . Acts 15:5: "But there rose up certain of the sect of the Pharisees which believed, saying, That it was needful to circumcise them, and to command them to keep the law of Moses."
   B. Upholders of traditions.
      1. Mark 7:3: "For the Pharisees, and all the Jews, except they wash their hands oft, eat not, holding the tradition of the elders."
      2. Mark 7:5-8: "Then the Pharisees and scribes asked him, Why walk not thy disciples according to the tradition of the elders, but eat bread with unwashen hands? He answered and said unto them, Well hath Esaias prophesied of you hypocrites, as it is written, This people honoureth me with their lips, but their heart is far from me. Howbeit in vain do they worship me, teaching for doctrines the commandments of men, For laying aside the commandment of God, ye hold the tradition of men, as the washing of pots and cups: and many other such like things ye do."
      3. Galatians 1:14: "And profited in the Jews' religion above many my equals in mine own nation, being more exceedingly zealous of the traditions of my fathers."
   C. Sticklers for Mosaic law.
      1. Acts 26:5: "Which knew me from the beginning, if they would testify, that after the most straitest sect of our religion I lived a Pharisee."
      2. Philippians 3:5: "Circumcised the eighth day, of the stock of Israel, of the tribe of Benjamin, an Hebrew of the Hebrews; as touching the law, a Pharisee."
   D. Very careful in outward details.
      1. Matthew 23:23: "Woe unto you, scribes and Pharisees, hypocrites! for ye pay tithe of mint and anise and cummin, and have omitted the weightier matters of the law, judgment, mercy, and faith: these ought ye to have done, and not to leave the other undone."

    2.   Luke 18:11: "The Pharisee stood and prayed thus with himself, God, I thank thee, that I am not as other men are, extortioners, unjust, adulterers, or even as this publican."

E. Rigid in fasting.
    1.   Luke 5:33: "And they said unto him, Why do the disciples of John fast often, and make prayers, and likewise the disciples of the Pharisees; but thine eat and drink?"
    2.   Luke 18:12: "I fast twice in the week, I give tithes of all that I possess."

F. Zealous for Judaism.
    1.   Matthew 23:15: "Woe unto you, scribes and Pharisees, hypocrites! for ye compass sea and land to make one proselyte, and when he is made, ye make him twofold more the child of hell than yourselves."

G. Lovers of display.
    1.   Matthew 23:5-7: "But all their works they do for to be seen of men: they make broad their phylacteries, and enlarge the borders of their garments, and love the uppermost rooms at feasts, and the chief seats in synagogues. And greetings in the markets to be called of men, Rabbi, Rabbi."

H. Covetous.
    1.   Luke 16:14: "And the Pharisees also, who were covetous, heard all these things: and they derided him."

———————— O ————————

INTERPRETATION OUTLINE

"Pharisees" (Sample No. 2)
Student Sample

I. Cruel persecutors
    A. Acts 9:1,2: "And Saul, yet breathing out threatenings and slaughter against the disciples of the Lord, went unto the high priest, and desired of him letters to

Damascus to the synagogues, that if he found any of this way, whether they were men or women, he might bring them bound unto Jerusalem."

B. Philippians 3:5,6: "Circumcised the eighth day, of the stock of Israel, of the tribe of Benjamin, an Hebrew of the Hebrews; as touching the law, a Pharisee; Concerning zeal, persecuting the church; touching the righteousness which is in the law, blameless."

II. Chief errors of their:
A. Outward righteousness
1. Luke 7:36-50: "And one of the Pharisees desired him that he would eat with him. And he went into the Pharisee's house, and sat down to meat. And, behold, a woman in the city, which was a sinner, when she knew that Jesus sat at meat in the Pharisee's house, brought an alabaster box of ointment. And stood at his feet behind him weeping, and began to wash his feet with tears, and did wipe them with the hairs of her head, and kissed his feet, and anointed them with the ointment. Now when the Pharisee which had bidden him saw it, he spake within himself, saying, This man, if he were a prophet, would have known who and what manner of woman this is that toucheth him: for she is a sinner. And Jesus answering said unto him, Simon, I have somewhat to say unto thee. And he saith, Master, say on. There was a certain creditor which had two debtors: the one owed five hundred pence, and the other fifty. And when they had nothing to pay, he frankly forgave them both. Tell me therefore, which of them will love him most? Simon answered and said, I suppose that he, to whom he forgave most. And he said unto him, Thou hast rightly judged. And he turned to the woman, and said unto Simon, Seest thou this woman? I entered into thine house, thou gavest me no water for my feet: but she hath washed my feet with tears, and wiped them with the hairs of her head. Thou gavest me no kiss: but this woman

since the time I came in hath not ceased to kiss my feet. My head with oil didst thou not anoint: but this woman hath anointed my feet with ointment. Wherefore I say unto thee, her sins which are many, are forgiven; for she loved much: but to whom little is forgiven, the same loveth little. And he said unto her, Thy sins are forgiven. And they that sat at meat with him began to say within themselves, Who is this that forgiveth sins also? And he said to the woman, Thy faith hath saved thee; go in peace."

B. Blindness to spiritual things

   1. John 3:1-10: "There was a man of the Pharisees, named Nicodemus, a ruler of the Jews: The same came to Jesus by night, and said unto him, Rabbi, we know that thou art a teacher come from God: for no man can do these miracles that thou doest, except God be with him, Jesus answered and said unto him, Verily, verily, I say unto thee, Except a man be born again, he cannot see the kingdom of God. Nicodemus saith unto him, How can a man be born when he is old? can he enter the second time into his mother's womb, and be born? Jesus answered, Verily, verily, I say unto thee, Except a man be born of water and of the Spirit, he cannot enter into the kingdom of God. That which is born of flesh is flesh; and that which is born of the Spirit is spirit. Marvel not that I said unto thee, Ye must be born again. The wind bloweth where it listeth, and thou hearest the sound thereof, but canst not tell whence it cometh, and whither it goeth: so is every one that is born of the Spirit. Nicodemus answered and said unto him, How can these things be? Jesus answered and said unto him, Art thou a master of Israel, and knowest not these things?"

C. Emphasis on the ceremonial law

   1. Matthew 15:1-9: "Then came to Jesus scribes and Pharisees, which were of Jerusalem saying, Why do thy disciples trangress the tradition of the elders? for they wash not their hands when they

eat bread. But he answered and said unto them,
Why do ye also transgress the commandment of
God by your tradition? For God commanded saying, Honour thy father and mother: and, he that
curseth father or mother, let him die the death.
But ye say, Whosoever shall say to his father or his
mother, it is a gift, by whatsoever thou mightest
be profited by me; And honour not his father and
his mother, he shall be free, Thus have ye made
the commandment of God of none effect by your
tradition. Ye hypocrites, well did Esaias prophesy
of you saying, This people draweth nigh unto me
with their mouth, and honoureth me with their
lips; but their heart is far from me. But in vain
they do worship me, teaching for doctrines the
commandments of men."

D. Perversion of Scripture
  1. Matthew 15:1,9: "Then came to Jesus scribes and
     Pharisees, which were of Jerusalem." "But in vain
     they do worship me, teaching for doctrines the
     commandments of men."

E. Hindering potential believers
  1. Acts 9:16,22: "For I will shew him how great
     things he must suffer for my name's sake." "But
     Saul increased the more in strength, and con-
     founded the Jews which dwelt at Damascus, prov-
     ing that this is very Christ."

INTERPRETATION OUTLINE

John 4
"Worship"
Student Sample

I. Old Testament use
  A. Meaning of word in Hebrew
    1. "Service, labor of slaves, hired servants"

B. Method
  1. Public praise: Psalm 92:95-100
  2. Congregational praise: Psalm 42:4; 1 Chronicles 9:20
  3. Individuals: Genesis 24:26; Exodus 33:9; 34:8
  4. Prayer: Psalms 60:79,80
  5. Three-fold emphasis:
    a. prayers
    b. Scripture reading
    c. exposition

C. Purpose: To express one's love and gratitude to God in a real act of inward spiritual worship, Deuteronomy 11:13; tension existed between ceremonial and spiritual aspect, Exodus 40:6

II. Worship in New Testament
A. Its nature: two aspects of one kind of worship
  1. In spirit: John 4:24 (Phil. 3:3) not where, but how
    a. spiritual worship—opposite of mere external rites; flesh
      1) God is spirit
      2) need spiritual birth, John 3:5, 6
      3) not confined to place or position!
    b. must—absolute necessity
      1) Spirit, John 3:7
      2) Atonement, John 3:15
      3) Worship, John 4:24
    c. today: fleshly rather than spiritual; external spectacular rather than internal and reverential, Matthew 15:8, 9ff; the heart, John 2:24 and John 3; heart darkened, Romans 1
    d. Romans 8—flesh, spirit.
    e. God is spirit, light, love but not spirit, love, light is God-word order
  2. In truth
    a. according to truth, in a manner suitable to His self-revelation.
    Holy Spirit-truth
    Word-truth; knowledge of truth
    Jesus Christ-truth
    Romans 2:1-3 (not what you thought)

  b. reality
  c. knowledge-John 22 (23, 24 truth); Revelation
    22:9, "Keep words of this book"; it does matter
    that we have a true conception of God.
  d. true worshipper
    1) If worship in Jerusalem does not mean
      true worship
    2) If worship in Samaria does not mean true
      worship
    3) True worship is spirit and truth
  e. truly also not in pretense, but sincerely
 B. Its manifestation/mechanics
  1. Praise: Ephesians 5:19—"Gratitude seems fun-
    damental nature"
    a. hymns: Revelation 5:8-14; 1 Corinthians
      14:26; Colossians 3:16
    b. psalms: Colossians 3:16; Matthew 26:30
    c. joy: rises spontaneously from basic mood of
      joy. "Close fellowship with one who is prais-
      ed." "In commanding us to glorify Him, God is
      inviting us to enjoy Him," C. S. Lewis, *Reflec-
      tion*, p. 98.
  2. Prayer
  3. Fasting
  4. Use—reading and expanding the Word
  5. Languages: 1 Corinthians 14
  6. Love feast: 1 Corinthians 11:23-25
  7. Service to fellow man: Luke 10:25-42; Matthew
    5:23-48; James 1:23
  8. Dedication: Romans 12:1
 C. Misconceptions of worship
  1. External rites: Romans 2:17-3:8; Matthew 15:8, 9
  2. Sincere: Romans 2:1-16

III. Misuse of worship
 A. Heathen have capacity: Romans 1; Revelation 13:8
  Heart darkened-no true worship
 B. Who?
  1. Heathen: Romans 1
  2. Moral man: Romans 2:1-16
  3. Religious man: Romans 2:17-3:8

C. How?
1. Pride: Romans 1
2. Ceremonial
3. Wrong object: Romans 1; John 4; Revelation 13:8
4. In the flesh
5. Not of the truth (Samaria)
6. Not a perfected or pure conscience: Hebrews 9:9-14 Simple block—purify conscience, true worship implies a knowledge of forgiveness of sins.
7. "Soulish"; emotional, five senses, atmosphere, temple of Salome, nature, etc.

IV. Time of worship
A. Day: Acts 20:7
B. Daily: Acts 2:46

V. Emphasis of worship: Inner love and devotion of the heart, gratitude

---

θ

INTERPRETATION OUTLINE

John 1:1-5
Student Sample

I. Whole passage - John 1:1-5
A. English translations
1. *New American Standard Bible:* "In the beginning was the Word, and the Word was with God, and the Word was God. He was in the beginning with God. All things came into being by Him, and apart from Him nothing came into being that has come into being. In Him was life, and the life was the light of men. And the light shines in the darkness, and the darkness did not comprehend it."
2. *King James Version:* "In the beginning was the Word, and the Word was with God, and Word was God. The same was in the beginning with God. All things were made by Him; and without Him

was not anything made that was made. In Him was life, and the life was the light of men. And the light shineth in darkness; and the darkness comprehended it not."

3. *Revised Standard Version:* "In the beginning was the Word, and the Word was with God, and the Word was God. He was in the beginning with God; all things were made through Him, and without Him was not anything made that was made. In Him was life and the life was the light of men. The light shines in the darkness, and the darkness has not overcome it."

B. Greek-English translation
1. *Interlinear Greek-English New Testament:* "In [the] beginning was the Word, and the Word was with - God, and God was the Word. This one was in [the] beginning with - God. All things through him became, and without him became not one thing which has become. In him life was, and the life was the light of men; and the light in the darkness shines, and the darkness it not overtook."

C. Paraphrase
1. *The Living Bible:* "Before anything else existed, there was Christ, with God. He has always been alive and is Himself God. He created everything there is — nothing exists that He didn't make. Eternal life is in Him, and this life gives light to all mankind. His life is the light that shines through the darkness — and the darkness can never extinguish it."

D. Commentaries
1. *Halley:* "This sublime passage reminds us of the opening words of Genesis. Jesus is here expressly called 'God' and Creator. John is very positive that Jesus was a Personality existing from eternity. Jesus spoke of 'the glory he had with the Father before the world was (John 17:5),' as if longing to return to his homeland from what was to him a sojourn in a dreary world. One of the implications of Jesus' name as 'the Word' is that he was God's ex-

pression of Himself to mankind. One of the ideas in the word 'Light' as applied to Jesus is that it is He who makes clear the meaning and destiny of human existence." *Bible Handbook*, p. 471.

2. *Unger:* "These verses declare six great truths concerning our Lord Jesus Christ. (1) He was and is the Eternal One, who always existed before time and matter: 'In the beginning was the Word.' (2) He was and is a Person distinct from God the Father: 'The Word [the preincarnate Christ] was with God (the Father).' (3) He was and is God: 'The Word was God' (:1). (4) He was co-existent with God (the Father) from eternity (:2). (5) He was the Creator of the universe (:3). (6) He is the Source of all life and light (both physical and spiritual) (:4, 5)." *Bible Handbook*, p. 546.

II. Each verse found in John 1:1-5
A. "In the beginning was the Word and the Word was with God and the Word was God (:1)."
    1. "Three great facts are made known concerning our Lord. (1) He is eternal. He did not begin to exist. He has no beginning, for 'in the beginning *was* the Word.' He ever was. Before time began and matter was created, He was. (2) He was and is a Person distinct from God the Father, yet one with Him, 'The Word was with God.' (3) The Lord Jesus Christ *is* God, for we read, 'The Word was God.'" *The Annotated Bible*, p. 187.
    2. Each phrase found in John 1:1.
        a. "In the beginning was the Word"
            1) The phrase "in the beginning (Greek, *en archēi)* seems to refer to a point in time in eternity past beyond which it is impossible for us to go, as I. A. Dorner interprets it. The verb is also chosen to state eternity as the word "was" (Greek, *ēn)* implies continued existence. As Marcus Dods states, "The *Logos* did not then begin to be, but at that point at which all else began to be He

already was." John Walvoord, *Jesus Christ Our Lord*, p. 24.

    2) Other verses
      a) Genesis 1:1
      b) Colossians 1:17
      c) John 8:58
      d) John 17:5
      e) Philippians 2:6
      f) John 17:24
      g) Micah 5:2

  b. "The Word was with God."
    1) Co-existence with God
    2) Other verses
      a) 1 John 1:1
      b) 1 John 1:2
      c) John 17:5

  c. "The Word was God."
    1) "The Word was with God, in respect of essence and substance, for the Word was God: a distinct person or substance, for He was with God; and yet the same in substance, for he was God." *Matthew Henry Commentary*, p. 848.
    2) Other verses
      a) Isaiah 9:6
      b) Matthew 1:23
      c) John 20:28
      d) Romans 9:5
      e) Colossians 2:9
      f) Titus 2:13
      g) Hebrews 1:8
      h) 2 Peter 1:1
      i) 1 John 5:20
      j) Philippians 2:6
      k) Hebrews 1:9

B. "He was in the beginning with God" (John 1:2).
  1. Read notes on "a" under II.
C. "All things came into being through Him; and apart from Him nothing came into being that has come into being" (John 1:3).
  1. "If Christ is eternal, it also is obvious that He is

the uncaused cause, the self-existent One. As the Creator of all things, He Himself must be uncreated." John Walvoord, *Jesus Christ Our Lord*, p. 28.

2. Jesus has to be God, because God is the only Creator (Isaiah 44:24, Ephesians 3:9).

3. Other verses
   a. John 1:10
   b. 1 Corinthians 8:6
   c. Colossians 1:16
   d. Hebrews 1:2
   e. Hebrews 1:10

D. "In Him was life; and the life was the light of men (John 1:4)."

1. "This further proves that He is God, and every way qualified for his undertaking; for (1) He has life in Himself; not only the true God, but the living God. God is life; he swears by Himself when he saith, 'As I live.' (2) All living creatures have their life in him; not only all the matter of creation was made by Him, but all the life too, that is in the creation is derived from Him and supported by Him." *Matthew Henry Commentary*, p. 849.

2. Jesus has to be God because only God has life in Himself (John 5:26).

3. Other verses
   a. John 5:26
   b. John 11:25
   c. John 14:6

E. "And the light shines in the darkness; and the darkness did not comprehend it" (John 1:5).

1. "The eternal Word, as God, shines in the darkness of natural conscience." *Matthew Henry Commentary*, p. 849.

2. "By darkness, here may be understood: (1) The heathen world (Ephesians 5:8), (2) the Jewish people, (3) the fallen spirit of man." *Clarke's Commentary*, p. 512.

3. Other verses
   a. John 3:19

III. The term "Word" used by John in John 1:1:

SAMPLES

A. Bible dictionaries
1. *Unger:* "A term used by St. John conveying most expressively the mission of Jesus as the Revealer of the Godhead. The title declares Christ's eternity and absolute deity. Words are the vehicle for the revelation of the thoughts and intents of the mind to others. In the Person of the incarnate *Logos,* God has made Himself fully known to man...Christ as the Word of God constitutes the complete and ultimate divine revelation...The question of whether John was influenced by Philo and Alexandreian Greek speculation is frequently debated. It is preferable to see the origin of his thought in the Old Testament where the Word of God is the divine agent in creation and the revelation of God's will to men. Moreover, studies in the Dead Sea Scrolls have led a number of scholars to the conclusion that the background of John is Jewish rather than Hellenistic. John further discourses profoundly on the Person and work of "the Word" in his first Epistle (1:1, 5, 7) and finally in Revelation (19:13)" (*Bible Dictionary,* p. 664).
2. *Funk and Wagnalls:* "The Word, according to John is neither a figurative personification of the Divine reason and self-expression, nor an equivalent of the Memra. The term is used rather to identify the Messiah as a Divine Person pre-existing in eternity and becoming incarnate in Jesus Christ; in other words, the resemblances between the Philonian and the Johannine conceptions belong to the outward garb and vehicle of the thought, the inner core of which is different in each case. Whereas the *Logos* of Philo is a personified representation of the Divine reason, revealing the Godhead to man, the Johannine Word is the eternal Son of God, incarnated as the Redeemer of man from sin. No less a means of revelation, but much more than a revealer a person in the Godhead" (*A New Standard Bible Dictionary,* p. 952).

3. "Logos signifies in classical Greek both 'reason'
    and 'word.' Though in biblical Greek the term is
    mostly employed in the sense of 'word,' we can-
    not properly dissassociate the two significations.
    Every word implies a thought. It is impossible to
    imagine a time when God was without thought.
    Hence, thought must be eternal as the deity. The
    term 'thought' is probably the best equivalent for
    the Greek term, since it denotes, on the one
    hand, the faculty of reason, or the thought in-
    wardly conceived in the mind; and on the other
    hand, the thought outwardly expressed through
    the vehicle of language. The two ideas, thought
    and speech are indubitably blended in the term
    'Logos'" (*The International Standard Bible En-
    cyclopedia*, pp. 1911-1912).
4. "'The Word', meaning Christ, the wisdom and
    power of God and the first cause of all things;
    God's personal expression of Himself to man"
    (*The Living New Testament*, p. 214).

B. Secular dictionary
   1. "Logos: The divine word or reason incarnate in
      Jesus Christ. (Greek - a word, saying, speech,
      discourse, thought, proportion, ratio, reckoning
      akin to speech)" (*The Random House Dictionary
      of English Language*, p. 843).

C. Word studies
   1. *Vine*: "*Logos* denotes (I) the expression of
      thought—not the mere name of an object (a) as
      embodying a conception or an idea; (b) a saying or
      statement, (1) by God; (2) by Christ.
      (II) The Personal Word, a title of the Son of
      God; this identification is substantiated by the
      statements of doctrine in John 1:1-18, declaring
      in verses 1 and 2 (1) His distinct and superfinite
      Personality; (2) His relation in the Godhead; (3)
      His deity; in verse 3 His creative power.

      'Logos', the Word, the personal manifestation,
      not a part of the Divine nature, but of the whole
      deity.

      The title is used also in 1 John 1, 'the Word of

life,' combining the two declarations in John 1:1 and 4, and Revelation 19:13" (*Expository Dictionary of New Testament Words*, pp. 229-230).

2. *Vine:* "In John 1:1-3, Colossians 1:15-17, and Hebrews 1:2, 3, the special function of creating and upholding the universe is ascribed to Christ under His titles of Word, Image, Son, respectively. The kind of Creatorship so predicated of Him is not that of a mere instrument or artificer in the formation of the world, but that of 'One by whom, in whom, and for whom all things made, and through whom they subsist.' This implies the assertion of His true and absolute Godhood" (*Expository Dictionary of New Testament Words*, pp. 247-248).

D. Other verses where "the Word" is used.
   1. John 1:14 (the Word became flesh)
   2. 1 John 1:1
      a. Jesus is called the Word of life — what was from the beginning; what John had heard, seen, beheld and handled.
   3. Revelation 19:13
      a. Jesus is called the Word of God at His second coming.

LIST OF BASIC TRUTHS IN JOHN 3:1-8

Student Sample

1. Must be born again.
2. Natural man can't understand spiritual truth.
3. Natural man can't see Spirit.
4. Flesh & spirit are separate.
5. Like + like = like.
6. Jesus is God
7. Man is incomplete till he is born again.
8. Being religious not sufficient to enter kingdom of God.
9. Social and moral status not enough.
10. We don't accomplish rebirth ourselves.
11. Regenerated by Word of God.
12. Just believing Jesus as Son of God not sufficient.
13. Must be an initial purification.
14. Shouldn't be surprised.
15. Jesus came from God.
16. Jesus sensitive to individuals.
17. Humility to God greater than humility to men.
18. Led Nic. from his level to His level.
19. Christ knows men's hearts.
20. Birth from above equals permanent change in nature.
21. Heart of man must be changed.
22. Anyone can come to Christ day or night.
23. New birth is universal.
24. One way to kingdom of God.
25. Everyone has the potential to reach God.
26. Difference between seeing and entering kingdom.
27. Age and education are not requirements to enter kingdom of God.
28. Humility.
29. Know Scripture only is not enough.
30. Christ always stayed on a spiritual level.
31. Not everyone is a child of God
32. If you are sincere - God will reveal Himself.
33. Sincerity of belief is not enough to enter.
34. Jesus changes the heart of man, not environment.
35. We cannot change ourselves.
36. Recognition of Jesus as a great teacher and leader is not enough

SAMPLES

APPLICATION OUTLINE

John 4
Student Sample

I. *Basic truths*
   A. John 4:27-43; People are ready to hear now: aggressive evangelism vs. friendship evangelism.
      1. Woman, v. 29
      2. Men, vs. 39
      3. Many more men, vs. 41

II. *Application*
   A. Randoms
   B. People of other colors
   C. Coffee shops, book store, sport
   D. Free speech
      1. Freedom
      2. Problem
      3. Solutions
      4. Personal opportunity—pray-with-me invitation

III. *Changes in life*
   A. Message—direct presentation of Jesus.
   B. Share testimony more.
   C. Attitude—people are interested; God has prepared.
   D. Ask people to help me—"Give me to drink?"!!
   E. Conversation—secular to general spiritual, spiritual in general to specific.
   F. Go out of my way—break/be willing/long-standing traditions.
   G. "Message"—use Four Laws principle in developing the need/solution approach.
   H. First-encounter evangelism.

IV. *Carry out these changes*
   A. Contrast awareness.
   B. Sensitivity to Holy Spirit.
   C. Sensitivity to possible barriers.
   D. Pray specifically for people in places where I am going to go.

E. Testimony written out and memorized.
F. Greater knowledge of Jesus' method of witnessing.
G. No arguing — compliment, continue.
H. Share concept with three people and in a group.
I. Holy Spirit.

V. *Prayer*
   A. "Lord Jesus, make me instant in season and out of season in sharing the Good News with others."

VI. *Verse*
   A. John 4:35.

VII. *Illustration*
   A. Be instant in season and out of season — *awareness of opportunities*. This chapter might be titled: "What Christ did, and what the disciples did not do (under the same circumstances)." While they were bargaining for "empanadas," Christ was leading a harlot to salvation.

   When the disciples went into town to buy some "empanadas y chorizos," who did they first pass on the way? The woman! Was she interested? Was she seeking Christ? Did the disciples talk with her? Who else did they pass? Verse 28, the men of the city! Were they interested? Did the disciples talk to them? I doubt it. They were too prejudiced at this time.

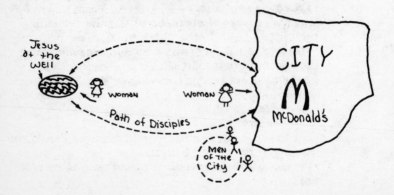

When the disciples returned to the well, who did they pass on the way? First, the men of the city. Did they talk to them? No. Second, they passed the woman returning to the city. Did they talk to her? No, and they chewed Christ out for having talked to her.

I wonder if the disciples would have reported what they had seen and heard about Christ (1 John 1:3) if the woman and the men would have shown interest? "While Christ brought blessing to the city, the disciples only brought business to the local stores."

APPLICATION OUTLINE

John 1:1-5
Student Sample

I. *What is a basic truth in this portion of Scripture?*
   A. Jesus was and is the Eternal one who always existed before time and matter.

II. *How does it apply to a campus situation? work? organization? neighborhood? nation?)?*
   A. Stress how God can be known personally because of the Lord Jesus. God became a man to seek for man. Also, who can know you better than Jesus Christ— the Creator—God who became like one of His created creatures. Also, "We know love by this, that He laid down His life for us," we do not have a high priest who cannot sympathize with our weaknesses, and "No man has seen God at any time. The only begotten God, who is in the bosom of the Father, He has explained Him."

III. *In view of these truths, what specific changes should you make in your life?*
   A. Fix my eyes more on Jesus "the author and perfecter of faith."

    B. Live in a relationship with Jesus that I can say
honestly: "For me to live is Christ."

    C. My message: tell the non-Christian that God can be
known personally, because Jesus Christ is the "Living
Word of God."

IV. *How do you propose to carry out these changes?*
    A. In sharing the Four Laws, show the uniqueness of
Jesus Christ.
    B. Study more after IBS on the Person of Jesus:
Christology.
    C. Memorize the Scripture which shows the deity of
Jesus.
    D. Let the Jehovah's Witnesses know Jesus.

V. *What is your personal prayer regarding these truths?*
    A. That I may always praise Jesus Christ as my own God
and Lord. Always remember that I was not "redeemed
with perishable things...but with *precious* blood."
Also, my life and very existence is through His grace
and my salvation is "not of myself."

VI. *What verse would you like to memorize which best sum-
marizes the truths of the passage?*
    A. John 1:1-5

VII. *Develop an illustration that will aid in the retention and
communication of these truths.*

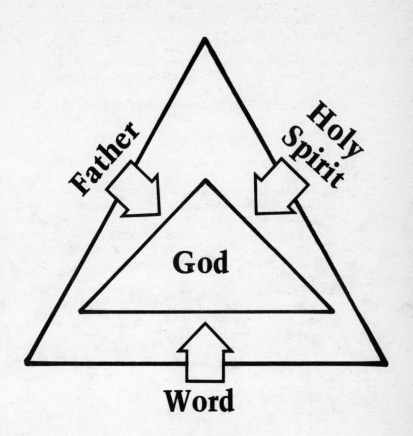

Annotated
Bibliography of
Bible Study
Helps

ANNOTATED BIBLIOGRAPHY OF BIBLE STUDY HELPS

Recommended Source Books for Research in Bible Study

The author would like to express his appreciation to Multnomah Press, publisher, and to James Braga, author, for the use of the list from *How To Study the Bible*.

Meaning of Words
(No Knowledge of Greek or Hebrew Necessary)

Old Testament

1. Unger, Merrill F.; and White, William Jr. *Nelson's Expository Dictionary of the Old Testament*. Nashville, Tennessee: Thomas Nelson, 1980.

For those who do not read Hebrew, this is probably the most helpful book giving meanings of Hebrew words. It makes an excellent companion volume to *Vine's Expository Dictionary of New Testament Words*.

2. Vine, W. E. *An Expository Dictionary of Old Testament Words*. Old Tappan, New Jersey: Fleming H. Revell Company, 1978.

Because of Vine's death, this work is incomplete. What there is, however, is helpful.

3. Wilson, William. *Wilson's Old Testament Word Studies*. Grand Rapids, Michigan: Kregel Publications.

Though the English reader can use this profitably, it is best used with some knowledge of Hebrew.

New Testament

1. Vine, W. E. *An Expository Dictionary of New Testament Words*.

Now available from several publishers, this book gives the meanings of Greek words, listing them alphabetically by their English translations.

KNOW YOUR BIBLE

Meanings of Words
(Some Knowledge of Greek or Hebrew Necessary)

Old Testament

1. Brown, F.; Driver, S. R.; and Briggs, C. A. *A Hebrew Lexicon of the Old Testament*. New York: Oxford University Press.

   This is the most authoritative lexicon of biblical Hebrew available today in English.

2. Davidson, Benjamin. *Analytical Hebrew and Chaldee Lexicon*. Grand Rapids, Michigan: Zondervan Publishing House.

   Gives parts of speech for words in the Hebrew Old Testament.

3. Holladay, William L. *A Concise Hebrew and Aramaic Lexicon of the Old Testament*. Grand Rapids, Michigan: Wm. B. Eerdmans Publishing Co., 1971.

   Although not as thorough as Brown, Driver, and Briggs, it presents a more concise, affordable alternative to the larger work.

New Testament

1. Arndt, W. F.; and Gingrich, F. W. *A Greek-English Lexicon of the New Testament*. Chicago: University of Chicago Press.

   This is the most authoritative lexicon of New Testament Greek available today in English.

2. Gingrich, F. W. *Shorter Lexicon of the Greek New Testament*. Chicago: University of Chicago Press, 1957.

   A conveniently sized lexicon which can be carried with your New Testament.

3. Lampe, G. W. H. *Patristic Greek Lexicon*. New York: Oxford University Press.

   This is the authoritative lexicon for Patristic (sacred post-New Testament) Greek.

4. Liddell, H. G.; and Scott, R. *Greek-English Lexicon.* New York: Oxford University Press, 1940.
 This is the authoritative lexicon for classical Greek.

5. Thayer, Joseph H. *Greek-English Lexicon of the New Testament.*
 This was once the standard. It is still quite useful, though not on a par with Arndt and Gingrich

6. _____. *Analytical Greek Lexicon.* Grand Rapids, Michigan: Zondervan Publishing House.
 This book gives the parts of speech for words in the Greek New Testament.

Concordances

Of English Translations: King James Version

1. Cruden, Alexander. *Cruden's Complete Concordance.*
 Though not exhaustive, this concordance meets the needs of most Bible students.

2. Strong, James. *Strong's Exhaustive Concordance of the Bible.*
 Every occurrence of every word in the KJV is listed

3. Young, Robert. *Analytical Concordance to the Bible.*
 This book and Strong's are the two most complete for the KJV.

Of English Translations: Revised Standard Version

1. Morrison, Clinton. *An Analytical Concordance to the Revised Standard Version of the New Testament.* Philadelphia: Westminster Press.

2. *Nelson's Complete Concordance of the Revised Standard Version.* 2nd ed. Nashville: Thomas Nelson, Inc.

Of English Translations: New American Standard Bible

1. Thomas, Robert. *New American Standard Exhaustive Concordance to the Bible.* Nashville: A. J. Holman Co., 1981.

Of English Translations: New International Version

1. Goodrick, E. W.; and Kohlenberger, J. R. *NIV Complete Concordance.* Grand Rapids, Michigan: Zondervan Publishing House, 1981.

Other English Translations

1. Darton, Michael. *Modern Concordance to the New Testament.* Garden City, New York: Doubleday & Co., Inc. 1976.
   This concordance is designed to be used with six different English versions.

Of the Hebrew Old Testament

1. Lisowsky, Gerhard. *Koncordanz zum Hebraischen Alten Testament.* Available through the American Bible Society.
   This book lists every occurrence of the Hebrew word, along with its context in the Hebrew Old Testament. What's not in Hebrew in this volume is in German.

2. Wigram, George. *Englishman's Hebrew and Chaldee Concordance.* Grand Rapids, Michigan: Zondervan Publishing House.
   This book lists every occurrence of the Hebrew word, along with its context in the King James Version.

Of the Greek New Testament

1. Moulton, J. H.; and Geden, G. *Concordance to the Greek New Testament.* Grand Rapids, Michigan: Kregel Publications.
   This book lists every occurrence of the Greek word, along with its context in the Greek New Testament.

2. Wigram, George. *Englishman's Greek Concordance of the New Testament.* Grand Rapids, Michigan: Zondervan Publishing House.
   This book lists every occurrence of the Greek word, along with its context in the King James Version.

▼ APPENDIX ▼
ANNOTATED BIBLIOGRAPHY OF BIBLE STUDY HELPS

Word Studies

Old Testament

1. Botterweck, G. J.; and Ringgren, H. *Theological Dictionary of the Old Testament*. Grand Rapids, Michigan: Wm. B. Eerdmans Publishing Co.

   This set of twelve (projected) volumes, though somewhat technical, is an authoritative source of information on Hebrew words.

2. Harris, R.; Archer, Gleason L.; and Waltke, Bruce K. *Theological Wordbook of the Old Testament*. Chicago: Moody Press, 1981.

   Though far more concise and limited than the *Theological Dictionary of the Old Testament*, it is probably more usable by the average Bible student, especially those who also use Strong's Concordance, to which this two-volume set is keyed.

New Testament

1. Barclay, William. *New Testament Words*. Philadelphia: Westminster Press, 1974.

   This little book has always fascinating and usually (but not always) accurate information about many New Testament words.

2. Brown, Colin. *Dictionary of New Testament Theology*. Grand Rapids, Michigan: Zondervan Publishing House, 1976.

   This three-volume set does much of what Kittel does, but in a more concise and economical manner.

3. Bullinger, E. W. *Figures of Speech Used in the Bible*. Grand Rapids, Michigan: Baker Book House, 1968.

   This book describes scores of literary devices used in the Bible, giving examples of them.

4. Earle, Ralph. *Word Meanings in the New Testament*. Kansas City, Missouri: Beacon Hill Press.

   This is a fairly simple, easy-to-read set. Earle leans heavily on the work of others. Useful, if not very original.

5. Kittel, Gerhard. *Theological Dictionary of the New Testament.* Grand Rapids, Michigan: Wm. B. Eerdmans Publishing Co., 1964-76.

This ten-volume set is a standard of scholarship on Greek words of theological significance.

6. Moulton, J. H.; and Milligan, George. *The Vocabulary of the Greek New Testament.* Grand Rapids, Michigan. Wm. B. Eerdmans Publishing Co., 1930.

This book illustrates how words in the New Testament were used in non-Biblical sources.

7. Robertson, A. T. *Word Pictures in the New Testament.* Nashville: Broadman Press, 1943.

This six-volume set is more technical and more useful than Wuest's or Vincent's.

8. Vincent, M. R. *Word Studies in the New Testament.* Grand Rapids, Michigan: Wm. B. Eerdmans Publishing Co., 1957.

This work is not as detailed as Robertson's, but is still quite useful. It provides a commentary on the New Testament.

9. Wuest, Kenneth. *Word Studies in the Greek New Testament.* Grand Rapids, Michigan: Wm. B. Eerdmans Publishing Co.

Although poorly edited and indexed, this set is nevertheless quite helpful. It provides a commentary on many books of the New Testament.

Bible Dictionaries and Encyclopedias

One-Volume Dictionaries

1. Bryant, Alton. *New Compact Bible Dictionary.* Grand Rapids, Michigan: Zondervan Publishing House, 1967.

Although this is not nearly as extensive as the others listed here, it is the best of the small Bible dictionaries. A paperback is available at a very reasonable price.

2. Douglas, J. D. *New Bible Dictionary.* Grand Rapids, Michigan: Wm. B. Eerdmans Publishing Co., 1962.

Although this is out of print, it is still the finest single-volume Bible dictionary around.

3. Tenney, Merrill C. *Zondervan Pictorial Bible Dictionary*. Grand Rapids, Michigan: Zondervan Publishing House, 1969.

Probably the best one-volume Bible dictionary still in print. More than half the pages have some illustration on them.

4. Unger, Merrill F. *Unger's Bible Dictionary*. Chicago: Moody Press, 1957.

This popular work is very helpful, but could use revision in some articles.

Multi-volume Encyclopedias

1. Bromiley, Geoffrey W. *International Standard Bible Encyclopedia*, rev. ed. Grand Rapids, Michigan: Wm. B. eerdmans Publishing Co., 1979.

Volumes 1 and 2 set a high standard for this work, which, when completed, will be among the finest available.

2. Buttrick, George Arthur. *Interpreter's Dictionary of the Bible*. Nashville: Abingdon Press, 1962.

This four-volume set, plus the supplementary volume (1976), which updates the set, is an excellent one, especially in matters of geography, history, and culture. It is liberal in theology.

3. Douglas, J. D. *Illustrated Bible Dictionary*. Wheaton, Illinois: Tyndale House Publishers, 1981.

The text is a revision of the *New Bible Dictionary*. The illustrations are lavish, well chosen, and helpful. This is a lovely three-volume set.

4. Orr, James. *International Standard Bible Encyclopedia*. Grand Rapids, Michigan: Wm. B. Eerdmans Publishing Co.

This work was the standard for years, and many of its articles are still unsurpassed. However, because it is dated, it is now being fully revised.

5. Pfeiffer, C. F.; Vos, H. F.; and Rea, John. *Wycliffe Bible Encyclopedia*. Chicago: Moody Press, 1975.

A fine two-volume set that is concise, but complete.

6. Tenney, Merrill C. *Zondervan Pictorial Bible Encyclopedia*. Grand Rapids, Michigan: Zondervan Publishing House, 1974.

This five-volume set is to be ranked at or near the top.

Bible Handbooks

1. Alexander, David; and Alexander, Pat. *Eerdman's Handbook to the Bible*. Grand Rapids, Michigan: Wm. B. Eerdmans Publishing Co., 1973.

This is the best of the Bible handbooks, both in terms of text and its lovely instructive illustrations.

2. Beers, V. Gilbert. *Victor Handbook of Bible Knowledge*. Wheaton, Illinois: Victor Books, 1981.

This is a family book giving background and exposition of most major events in Scripture, arranged in biblical order. The illustrations appeal to young and old alike.

3. Halley, Henry H. *Halley's Bible Handbook*. Grand Rapids, Michigan: Zondervan Publishing House.

4. Unger, Merrill F. *Unger's Bible Handbook*. Chicago: Moody Press, 1966.

Unger's and Halley's are very similar. It is amazing how much information can be packed into such small volumes. Either book provides an economical alternative to Eerdman's.

Bible Atlases

1. Aharoni, Y.; and Avi-Yonah, M. *Macmillan Bible Atlas*, rev. ed. New York: Macmillan Publishing Co., Inc., 1977.

This is generally considered the best. It has many (264) maps which portray virtually every biblical event that can be depicted cartographically.

2. Frank, Harry Thomas. *Hammond's Atlas of the Bible Lands*. Wheaton, Illinois: Scripture Press, 1977.

ANNOTATED BIBLIOGRAPHY OF BIBLE STUDY HELPS

A reasonable priced paperback atlas with maps which do a better than average job of showing topography.

3. May, Herbert G. *Oxford Bible Atlas*. New York: Oxford University Press, 1974.
This has an excellent index to the maps.

4. Monson, J. *Student Map Manual: Historical Geography of the Bible Lands*. Grand Rapids, Michigan: Zondervan Publishing House, 1979.
Has the most detailed maps of these Bible atlases, along with excellent indexes, cross-references, and space for notes. Uses the biblical eastward orientation. Limited to Palestine.

5. Wright, G. E.; and Filson, Floyd V. *Westminster Historical Atlas to the Bible*. Philadelphia: Westminster Press, 1956.
Very large maps, with great detail — possibly too cluttered.

6. *Compact Bible Atlas with Gazetteer*. Grand Rapids, Michigan: Baker Book House, 1979.
Because of its small size, it is most convenient to carry. Has the same maps as the Hammond's, but a better index.

Bible Introduction

Old Testament

1. Archer, Gleason, *Survey of Old Testament Introduction*. Chicago: Moody Press, 1973.
A good standard textbook. It is semi-technical, perhaps too difficult for some beginners.

2. Bullock, C. Hassel. *An Introduction to the Old Testament Poetic Books*. Chicago: Moody Press, 1979.
A very fine work on the books of this particular literary genre. Of medium difficulty.

3. Freeman, Hobart E. *An Introduction to the Old Testament Prophets*. Chicago: Moody Press.
An excellent work on these biblical books. This makes a good companion volume to Bullock's work.

4. Harrison, R. K. *Introduction to the Old Testament.* Grand Rapids, Michigan: Wm. B. Eerdmans Publishing Co., 1969.

Though excellent, this work is quite technical, and probably not the best for beginners.

5. Jensen, Irving C. *Jensen's Survey of the Old Testament.* Chicago: Moody Press, 1978.

This work makes excellent use of charts and a basic text. It is very good for a basic Old Testament introduction and survey.

6. Mears, Henrietta. *What the Bible Is All About.* Ventura, California: Gospel Light Publications, 1953.

This is a very simple volume, but can be of help to the beginning Bible student. It covers both Old and New Testaments.

7. Unger, Merrill F. *Introductory Guide to the Old Testament.* Grand Rapids, Michigan: Zondervan Publishing House, 1951.

Complete, but not too technical. Very good for beginners.

8. Young, Edward J. *Introduction to the Old Testament.* Grand Rapids, Michigan: Wm. B. Eerdmans Publishing Co., 1949.

A good standard textbook.

New Testament

1. Foulkes, Francis. *Pocket Guide to the New Testament.* Downers Grove, Illinois: InterVarsity Press, 1978.

A concise and very basic work. Includes study questions, topics for further study, and a brief bibliography.

2. Guthrie, Donald. *New Testament Introduction.* Downers Grove, Illinois: InterVarsity Press, 1970.

This volume, though perhaps too technical for some beginners, is probably the finest New Testament introduction.

3. Harrison, Everett F. *Introduction to the New Testament.* Grand Rapids, Michigan: Wm. B. Eerdmans Publishing Co., 1964.

A standard college-level text with good general New Testament introductory material, as well as individual book introductions.

4. Hiebert, D. Edmond. *Introduction to the New Testament*, 3 vol. Chicago: Moody Press, 1977.

Volume 1, The Gospels and Acts; Volume 2, The Pauline Epistles; Volume 3, The Non-Pauline Epistles and Revelation. This is an excellent set, covering the more technical introductory problems in a clear, non-technical manner. The work includes fine bibliographies on each biblical book.

5. Jensen, Irving L. *Jensen's Survey of the New Testament*. Chicago: Moody Press, 1981.

This work, like its Old Testament companion, is concise and easy to use, with excellent charts.

Bible Geography and History

1. Adams, J. McKee. *Biblical Backgrounds*. Nashville: Broadman Press, 1965.

More concise than Baly, Pfeiffer, or Smith, this book gives excellent historical information on many biblical areas, including those outside of Palestine.

2. Baly, Denis. *Geography of the Bible*. New York: Harper & Row, 1974.

Though some history is given, the emphasis is on the geography and climate. In these areas the book is unsurpassed. Limited to Palestine.

3. Bright, John. *A History of Israel*. Philadelphia: Westminster Press, 1972.

One of the finest Old Testament histories available, despite its acceptance of several liberal critical views.

4. Davis, John J.; and Whitcomb, John C. *A History of Israel: From Conquest to Exile*. Grand Rapids, Michigan: Baker Book House, 1980.

Originally published as three paperback volumes, this work covers the Old Testament period with a strong emphasis on the historical and archaeological backgrounds of that period.

5. Pfeiffer, Charles R.; and Vos, Howard F. *Wycliffe Historical Geography of Bible Lands*. Chicago: Moody Press, 1967.
A most excellent work giving information for not only Palestine, but all Old and New Testament lands of biblical significance. Well-written in non-technical language.

6. Smith, George Adam. *Historical Geography of the Holy Land*. Grand Rapids, Michigan: Kregel Publications.
A classic in this field, still considered by some to be the finest of its kind ever done.

7. Wood, Leon. *A Survey of Israel's History*. Grand Rapids, Michigan: Zondervan Publishing House, 1970.
This is a good book introducing the history of Israel in Old Testament times.

Bible Manners and Customs

1. Alexander, Patricia, ed. *Eerdman's Family Encyclopedia of the Bible*. Grand Rapids, Michigan: Wm. B. Eerdmans Publishing Co., 1978.
This beautiful volume gives much information on manners and customs in the most attractive and interesting format available. You can well leave this on your coffee table when not in use.

2. Bouquet, A. C. *Everyday Life in New Testament Times*. New York: Charles Scribner's Sons, 1953.
Very excellent volume, somewhat technical, on the physical anthropology of New Testament times.

3. de Vaux, Roland. *Ancient Israel*. New York: McGraw-Hill Book Co., 1965. Volume 1, Social Institutions; Volume 2, Religious Institutions.
This two-volume set is very complete and scholarly. It may be the most thorough treatment of the subject available at a reasonable price.

ANNOTATED BIBLIOGRAPHY OF BIBLE STUDY HELPS

4. Heaton, Eric W. *Everyday Life in Old Testament Times*. New York: Charles Scribner's Sons, 1977.
    Companion to Bouquet. Very good information, but possibly more technical than some would need.

5. Miller, Madeleine S.; and Miller, J. Lane. *Harper's Encyclopedia of Bible Life*. New York: Harper & Row, 1978.
    More complete than Wight, but might be a little wordy. Very helpful indexes, as well as suggestions for further reading.

6. Packer, J. I.; Tenney, Merrill C.; and White, William Jr. *The Bible Almanac*. Nashville: Thomas Nelson, Inc., 1980.
    This is a large volume packed with information on this subject. Not only is the text good, but the illustrations and index are very useful.

7. Wight, Fred H. *Manners and Customs of Bible Lands*. Chicago: Moody Press, 1953.
    This book deals topically with manners and customs in a simple, well-written manner.

8. Wright, G. Ernest, ed. *Great People of the Bible and How They Lived*. New York: Reader's Digest Association, 1974.
    This large and lavish volume has much good information on manners and customs, though Bible history seems to be its focus.

9. Specific articles on various topics (e.g. dress, houses, etc.) in any good Bible dictionary.

Archaeology

1. Kitchen, D. A. *The Bible in Its World*. Downers Grove, Illinois: InterVarsity Press, 1977.
    Kitchen ably brings archaeology to bear upon the various periods of Bible history.

2. Lewis, Jack P. *Archaeological Backgrounds to Bible People*. Grand Rapids, Michigan: Baker Book House, 1971.
    An informative book of what archaeology has contributed to the history of various persons mentioned in Scripture.

Originally titled *Historical Backgrounds of Bible History*.

3. Pfeiffer, Charles F. *The Biblical World: A Dictionary of Biblical Archaeology*. Grand Rapids, Michigan: Baker Book House, 1964.
    This volume alphabetically lists articles dealing with various aspects of biblical archaeology: places, persons, things, etc. An easy-to-use reference volume.

4. Schoville, Keith N. *Biblical Archaeology in Focus*. Grand Rapids, Michigan: Baker Book House.
    This book does a fine job of covering both the methods and the findings of biblical archaeology.

5. Unger, Merrill F. *Archaeology and the Old Testament*. Chicago: Moody Press, 1954.
    This has much helpful information on the subject, but it could use some updating now. There is only a small section dealing with the role of biblical archaeology.

6._____. *Archaeology of the New Testament*. Chicago: Moody Press, 1962.
    A companion to his work on the Old Testament. It also could use some updating.

7. Vos, Howard F. *Archaeology in Bible Lands*. Chicago: Moody Press, 1977.
    An excellent and complete text. The first 100 pages deal with the nature of biblical archaeology and the last 300 pages with a regional survey of the findings of archaeology.

8. _____. *Beginnings in Bible Archaeology*. Chicago: Moody Press, 1956.
    A good little introduction to the subject, with the emphasis on the discipline of biblical archaeology more than the findings of archaeology.

▼ APPENDIX ▼
ANNOTATED BIBLIOGRAPHY OF BIBLE STUDY HELPS

Commentaries

One Volume

1. Church, Leslie F., ed. *Matthew Henry's Commentary on the Whole Bible.* Grand Rapids, Michigan: Zondervan Publishing House, 1961.

If you want an inspirational, devotional commentary in one volume, this is probably the best. But if you want something that explains the meaning of the text, get something else.

2. Guthrie, D.; Moyer, J. A.; Stibbs, A. M.; and Wiseman, D. J. *The New Bible Commentary*, rev. ed. Grand Rapids, Michigan: Wm. B. Eerdmans Publishing Co., 1970.

Very helpful whole-Bible commentary, which tends to be a bit more synthetic in its approach than the Wycliffe.

3. Howley, G. C. D.; Bruce, F. F.; and Ellison, H. L. *The New Layman's Bible Commentary.* Grand Rapids, Michigan: Zondervan Publishing House, 1979.

May be the best of this group. Has helpful, essentially verse-by-verse commentary, but also includes numerous introductory and background articles which are, for the most part, very good.

4. Pfeiffer, Charles F.; and Harrison, Everett F. *Wycliffe Bible Commentary*. Chicago: Moody Press, 1962.

A helpful expository commentary.

Sets or Series

1. Barclay, William. *Daily Study Bible*. Philadelphia: Westminster Press.

This eighteen-volume set on the New Testament is one of the most fascinating, due to the author's writing skill. There is also much valuable information in it, although the conservative reader will not always find Barclay's theology to his liking.

2. Bruce, F. F., gen. ed. *New International Commentary on the New Testament*. Grand Rapids, Michigan: Wm. B. Eerdmans Publishing Co.

Though somewhat technical, this series is so excellent that even the beginner should be aware of it. It is hard to find a more consistant level of high quality than in this eighteen-volume set.

3. Ellicott, Charles John. *Ellicott's Commentary on the Whole Bible*. Grand Rapids, Michigan: Zondervan Publishing House.
This set, first published in the last century, is still an insightful and reverential set of commentaries.

4. Gaebelein, Frank E., gen. ed. *The Expositor's Bible Commentary*. Grand Rapids, Michigan: Zondervan Publishing House.
This set (projected at twelve volumes) is an excellent one, based on the text of the NIV. The passages are dealt with in a clear expositional manner, with critical notes separate for more advanced readers.

5. Harrison, R. K., gen. ed. *New International Commentary on the Old Testament*. Grand Rapids, Michigan: Wm. B. Eerdmans Publishing Co.
This is the companion series to the *New International Commentary on the New Testament*, and is also of the same high level of excellence.

6. Jamieson, R.; Faussett, A. R.; and Brown, D. A. *Commentary: Critical, Experimental, and Practical*. Grand Rapids, Michigan: Wm. B. Eerdmans Publishing Co.
This set was first published in the 1800s, but it is also one of the better sets. A bit more technical than Ellicott.

7. Lange, Joseph P. *Commentary on the Holy Scriptures*. Grand Rapids, Michigan: Zondervan Publishing House.
This unique twelve-volume set is geared for every need and every level of reader. Each section of Scripture is handled three separate times, first critically and exegetically, then doctrinally, and finally, practically. It dates from the 1800s.

8. Tasker, R. V. G., gen. ed. *Tyndale New Testament Commentary Series*. Grand Rapids, Michigan: Wm. B. Eerdmans Publishing Co.

This twenty-volume paperback series is perhaps the best buy on a set of New Testament commentaries. A high level of conservative scholarship is maintained throughout the series.

9. Wiseman, D. J., gen. ed. *Tyndale Old Testament Commentaries*. Downers Grove, Illinois: InterVarsity Press.

This series (projected at twenty-four volumes) is comparable to the series by the same name on the New Testament. Most volumes are now available, and thus far the series is very good.

10. *Everyman's Bible Commentaries*. Chicago: Moody Press.

This series of small paperbacks (approximately forty) covers most books in the Bible. They are very basic and simple, but by top-notch scholars with excellent credentials.

Commentaries on Specific Books of the Bible

Quite often many of the finest commentaries are individual works on specific books of the Bible. Rather than list these here, we will suggest several sources of information about them.

• Many of the works previously cited include excellent bibliographies, some annotated. These can be of great help.
• Often a Christian leader (pastor, elder, teacher, etc.) will be able to recommend books that will match your area of interest with your level of scholastic ability.
• There are several books that list commentaries on the various books of the Bible, as well as other types of biblical research books. Such lists (as with this list) will tend to include the author's favorites and exclude those he does not prefer. They will also tend to be geared for a higher scholastic level than many readers of this book (often the seminarian). Nevertheless, they are quite useful, and we list several here.

1. Barber, Cyril J. *The Minister's Library*. Grand Rapids, Michigan: Baker Book House, 1974.

This is the largest and most complete work of this kind done by a conservative. The annotations are brief but helpful. Every few years the author issues a *Periodic Supplement*, which brings the work up to date.

2. Barker, Kenneth L.; and Waltke, Bruce K. *Bibliography for Old Testament Exposition and Exegesis.* Dallas, Texas: Dallas Theological Seminary, 1975.

Although there are no annotations, the compilers indicate by an asterisk what they consider most essential to the seminarian's library.

3. Goldingay, John. *Old Testament Commentary Survey.* Downers Grove, Illinois: InterVarsity Press, 1977.

Although this book can be quite helpful, it lists so many out-of-print books that it is at times frustrating.

4. Johnson, S. Lewis, Jr. *Bibliography for New Testament Exegesis and Exposition.* Dallas, Texas: Dallas Theological Seminary.

This work is geared more for the expositor than the exegete, and it has very brief comments on each title.

5. Thiselton, Anthony C. *New Testament Commentary Survey,* rev. by Don Carson. Downers Grove, Illinois: InterVarsity Press, 1977.

The companion volume to Goldingay. Both works lean toward rather technical commentaries.

Topical Indexes

1. *Holman Topical Concordance.* Nashville: A. J. Holman Co., 1973.

This book lists references according to subject, with each subject having subtopics in outline form.

2. Joy, Charles R. *Harper's Topical Concordance.* New York: Harper & Row, 1976.

This volume is quite similar to Holman's. However, because it is considerably more expensive, the Holman Concordance is probably the better choice.

3. Nave, Orville J. *Nave's Topical Bible.* Chicago: Moody Press, 1975.

Lists over 20,000 topics or subtopics, with over 100,000 Scripture references. This is the most popular of the "topical Bibles."

ANNOTATED BIBLIOGRAPHY OF BIBLE STUDY HELPS

4. Viening, Edward, ed. *Zondervan Topical Bible*. Grand Rapids, Michigan: Zondervan Publishing House, 1969.

About 21,000 topics and subtopics list over 100,000 Scripture references. This is very similar to Nave's both in design and in completeness.

5. Wharton, Gary. *The New Compact Topical Bible*. Grand Rapids, Michigan: Zondervan Publishing House, 1972.

If you don't mind flipping the pages of your Bible to read the references, this is the book to get. Though about 1/3 the size (and price) of *Nave's* or *Zondervan's*, it actually has more references in it than either of those volumes. Over 25,000 subtopics and well over 100,000 references are included.

From the book *How To Study the Bible* by James Braga, © 1982, Multnomah Press, Portland, OR 97266. Used by permission.

Samples of Material to be Reproduced

What we want to do now is lay out a simple framework of what we have covered. This will help you in two areas:

1. It will provide a structure by which you can go back and review this book. It will provide you with the "big picture" of the Bible study method and help you as you study the different chapters of this book and get the method under your belt.

2. The review also will give you an effective transferable tool, by which to study the Word, that incorporates the principles you have learned. You can use it as a guide as you study a book, or you can share it with others. After a while, the whole process will become second nature to you.

As you move through the steps, always remember that the amount of time you study will determine how far you get. Remember you are preparing for a lifetime of study.

▼ A P P E N D I X ▼
KNOW YOUR BIBLE

What is helpful with the method we have learned is that it is so flexible in its use. If you have a lot of time, you can go through all the steps. Or, you can for example, skip the horizontal and vertical charts and begin immediately with the steps of observation. If you do not have time at the moment to do all the steps of observation, just do some of them for now. Or, you can begin your study with the steps of interpretation. Or, if you are really pushed for time, start with application.

I suggest doing some application after various parts of your study. Do not wait to apply until you are finished with all the interpretation. Application can and should be woven in throughout your study.

The forms which appear on the following pages may be reproduced for your personal use. You also may find it helpful, as many others have, to remove the lists of questions and *glue them into the back of your Bible*. Then when you want to understand a passage of Scripture better, or when you have an opportunity to inject some light and direction into a group Bible study, these lists will be available for quick reference.

Step 1. Right mind set.
Step 2. Charting.
Step 3. Observation.
Step 4. Interpretation.
Step 5. Application.

BOOK CHART

Chapters	1	2	3	4	5	6	7
Chapter Titles							

BOOK CHART

Chapters	1	2	3	4	5	6	7
Chapter Titles							
Paragraph Titles							
Key Verse: Key Word:							

OBSERVATION CHART

Scripture	Observations	Interpretive Questions

CROSS-REFERENCE CHART

Cross-reference	Significance

OBSERVATION QUESTIONS
from
A GUIDE TO UNDERSTANDING YOUR BIBLE
by
Josh McDowell

The Six Biggies

1. Who?

2. What?

3. When?

4. Where?

5. Why?

6. How?

Relationship Questions

1. Are there things that are alike?

2. Are there things that are different?

3. Are there things that are repeated?

4. Is there cause and effect?

5. Is there movement from general to specific?

6. Is there a progression?

7. Are there any questions or answers?

8. Is there a problem and a solution?

9. Is there emphasis by space?

10. Are there connectors?

11. Are there any commands?

12. Are there any promises?

Cut out and glue   **in back of Bible.**

INTERPRETATION STEPS
from
A GUIDE TO UNDERSTANDING YOUR BIBLE
by
Josh McDowell

1. Cross-reference study
2. Context
3. Definitions

      Secular dictionary

      Bible dictionary
4. Translations, paraphrases
5. Reference and topical books
6. Summary and outline

APPLICATION STEPS

Basic truths

1 How does this truth apply to my life (at work? in my neighborhood? at home? in my nation? etc.)?

2 In view of this truth, what specific changes should I make in my life?

3 How do I propose to carry out these changes?

4 What is my personal prayer regarding this truth?

5 What verse (or verses) of Scripture would I memorize to best summarize this truth?

6 What illustration can I develop that will help me to retain this truth and communicate it to others? You might incorporate a graphic, a cartoon, a drawing, a story, or a poem.

Cut out and glue **in back of Bible.**

SIGNIFICANT WORDS TO LOOK FOR

1. Logical connectors:
   a. Contrast . . . . but (Ephesians 2:4)
      even though (Romans 1:21)
      much more (Romans 5:15)
      nevertheless (Romans 5:33)
      yet (Romans 5:8)
      although
      then
      otherwise (Romans 11:6)
   b. Comparison . . . . too (Ephesians 2:3)
      also (Ephesians 1:11)
      as (Ephesians 5:22)
      just as (Ephesians 4:32)
      so also (Ephesians 5:28)
      likewise (1 Peter 3:7)
      and
      like
   c. Correlatives . . . . as . . . so also (Ephesians 5:24)
      for . . . as (Ephesians 5:23)
      so . . . as (Ephesians 5:28)
   d. Reason . . . . because (Ephesians 2:4)
      for this reason . . . . (Ephesians 3:15)
      for this purpose (Ephesians 6:22)
      for (Ephesians 2:8)
      since (Colossians 1:4)
   e. Result . . . . so then (Ephesians 2:19)
      therefore (Ephesians 2:11)
      as a result (Ephesians 4:14)
      thus
      then
   f. Purpose/Result . . . . that (Ephesians 1:4)
      so that (Ephesians 1:18)
      in order that (Ephesians 4:28)
   g. Condition . . . . if (Ephesians 3:2)

2. Temporal or time connectors:
   now (Ephesians 2:2)
   until (Ephesians 4:13)
   when (Ephesians 1:20)
   before (Ephesians 1:4)
   after (Ephesians 1:13)
   while (Ephesians 1:16)
   since (Colossians 3:1)

3. Geographical connectors:
   where (Colossians 3:1)

Cut out and glue in back of Bible.